# PEOPLE OF
# THE DESERT
✢

TIME® LIFE BOOKS

*Other Publications:*

THE ART OF WOODWORKING
LOST CIVILIZATIONS
ECHOES OF GLORY
THE NEW FACE OF WAR
HOW THINGS WORK
WINGS OF WAR
CREATIVE EVERYDAY COOKING
COLLECTOR'S LIBRARY OF THE UNKNOWN
CLASSICS OF WORLD WAR II
TIME-LIFE LIBRARY OF CURIOUS AND UNUSUAL FACTS
AMERICAN COUNTRY
VOYAGE THROUGH THE UNIVERSE
THE THIRD REICH
THE TIME-LIFE GARDENER'S GUIDE
MYSTERIES OF THE UNKNOWN
TIME FRAME
FIX IT YOURSELF
FITNESS, HEALTH & NUTRITION
SUCCESSFUL PARENTING
HEALTHY HOME COOKING
UNDERSTANDING COMPUTERS
LIBRARY OF NATIONS
THE ENCHANTED WORLD
THE KODAK LIBRARY OF CREATIVE PHOTOGRAPHY
GREAT MEALS IN MINUTES
THE CIVIL WAR
PLANET EARTH
COLLECTOR'S LIBRARY OF THE CIVIL WAR
THE EPIC OF FLIGHT
THE GOOD COOK
WORLD WAR II
HOME REPAIR AND IMPROVEMENT
THE OLD WEST

*For information on and a full description of any of the
Time-Life Books series listed above, please call
1-800-621-7026 or write:*
Reader Information
Time-Life Customer Service
P.O. Box C-32068
Richmond, Virginia 23261-2068

This volume is one of a series that chronicles the history and culture of the Native Americans. Other books in the series include:

THE FIRST AMERICANS
THE SPIRIT WORLD
THE EUROPEAN CHALLENGE

*The Cover:* Against a backdrop of mesa and sky, a group of Navajo riders trek across the flat, sandy floor of Arizona's Canyon de Chelly, for hundreds of years the sacred refuge of these hardy people of the desert. The canyon has been occupied by a succession of Indian cultures for at least two millennia. Before the Navajo, the Hopi farmed the fertile valley bottom; and before everyone, the Anasazi—Navajo for the "ancient ones"—lived in shelters built into the canyon's soft sandstone walls.

# PEOPLE OF THE DESERT

✤

*by*
THE EDITORS
*of*
TIME-LIFE BOOKS

ALEXANDRIA, VIRGINIA

Time-Life Books is a division of Time Life Inc.,
a wholly owned subsidiary of
## THE TIME INC. BOOK COMPANY

## TIME-LIFE BOOKS

PRESIDENT: Mary N. Davis

MANAGING EDITOR: Thomas H. Flaherty
*Director of Editorial Resources:* Elise D. Ritter-Clough
*Executive Art Director:* Ellen Robling
*Director of Photography and Research:* John Conrad Weiser
*Editorial Board:* Dale M. Brown, Janet Cave, Roberta Conlan, Laura Foreman, Jim Hicks, Blaine Marshall, Rita Thievon Mullin, Henry Woodhead
*Assistant Director of Editorial Resources/Training Manager:* Norma E. Shaw

PUBLISHER: Robert H. Smith

*Associate Publisher:* Sandra Lafe Smith
*Editorial Director:* Russell B. Adams, Jr.
*Marketing Director:* Anne C. Everhart
*Director of Production Services:* Robert N. Carr
*Production Manager:* Marlene Zack
*Supervisor of Quality Control:* James King

Editorial Operations
*Production:* Celia Beattie
*Library:* Louise D. Forstall
*Computer Composition:* Deborah G. Tait (Manager), Monika D. Thayer, Janet Barnes Syring, Lillian Daniels
*Interactive Media Specialist:* Patti H. Cass

**Library of Congress Cataloging in Publication Data**
People of the desert/by the editors of Time-Life Books.
    p.  cm. — (The American Indians)
Includes bibliographical references and index.
    ISBN 0-8094-9412-4
    ISBN 0-8094-9413-2 (lib. bdg.)
    1. Indians of North America—Southwest, New— Social life and customs.
    I. Time-Life Books. II. Series.
E98.S7P385   1993                           92-22262
305.897'079—dc20                               CIP

## THE AMERICAN INDIANS

SERIES EDITOR: Henry Woodhead
*Series Administrator:* Jane Edwin

Editorial Staff for *People of the Desert*
*Senior Art Directors:* Dale Pollekoff (principal), Herbert H. Quarmby
*Picture Editor:* Susan V. Kelly
*Text Editors:* John Newton (principal), Stephen G. Hyslop
*Writers:* Robin Currie, Maggie Debelius
*Associate Editors/Research:* Kirk E. Denkler, Sharon V. Kurtz (principals), Marilyn Murphy Terrell
*Assistant Art Director:* Susan M. Gibas
*Senior Copy Coordinator:* Ann Lee Bruen
*Picture Coordinator:* David Beard
*Editorial Assistant:* Gemma Villanueva

*Special Contributors:* Amy Aldrich, George Constable, George G. Daniels, Marfé Ferguson Delano, Barbara C. Mallen, Lydia Preston, David S. Thomson (text); Jennifer Veech, Anne Whittle (research); Barbara L. Klein (index).

*Correspondents:* Elisabeth Kraemer-Singh (Bonn), Christine Hinze (London), Christina Lieberman (New York), Maria Vincenza Aloisi (Paris), Ann Natanson (Rome).

*General Consultant*
Frederick E. Hoxie is director of the D'Arcy McNickle Center for the History of the American Indian at the Newberry Library in Chicago. Dr. Hoxie is the author of *A Final Promise: The Campaign to Assimilate the Indians 1880-1920* and other works. He has served as a history consultant to the Cheyenne River and Standing Rock Sioux tribes, Little Big Horn College archives, and the Senate Select Committee on Indian Affairs. He is a trustee of the National Museum of the American Indian in Washington, D.C.

*Special Consultants*
Garrick and Roberta Glenn Bailey are scholars at the University of Tulsa where Garrick Bailey is Professor of Anthropology and his wife a Research Associate. Garrick Bailey specializes in cultural anthropology, focusing on ethnicity and the socio-cultural adaptation of the Indians of the Americas. Roberta Glenn Bailey, an ethnohistorian, focuses on the material culture of Indians of the Southwest and Guatemala. They are the coauthors of *A History of the Navajo: The Reservation Years* and *Historic Changes in the Navajo Occupation of the Northern Chaco Plateau.*

Keith H. Basso, Professor of Anthropology at the University of New Mexico, has spent much of his professional career studying and writing about the Apache. Among his books are *The Cibecue Apache* and *Western Apache Language and Culture: Essays in Linguistic Anthropology.* He has also written numerous chapters and articles on the subject for books and periodicals. Dr. Basso is a fellow of the American Anthropological Association and a member of the Board of Directors of the Association on American Indian Affairs and of the Board of Trustees of the National Museum of the American Indian.

Robert L. Bee is Professor of Anthropology at the University of Connecticut, specializing in social anthropology and the study of North American Indians. He has focused much of his research on the socio-cultural change among Native Americans in the 20th century and American Indian religious movements. Dr. Bee has been a steady contributor to periodicals and scholarly journals and, among his books, is the author of *The Yuma* and *The Politics of American Indian Policy.* He is a Fellow of the American Anthropological Association.

Henry F. Dobyns is Adjunct Professor of Anthropology at the University of Oklahoma. He has done extensive field research on tribes of the southwestern United States and for three decades has documented his studies in many books, periodicals, and scholarly journals. Among his books are *The Papago People,* and *The Pima-Maricopa.* Dr. Dobyns is a Fellow of the American Association for the Advancement of Science, the American Anthropological Association, and the Society for Applied Anthropology.

Alfonso Ortiz, Professor of Anthropology at the University of New Mexico, is the author of *The Tewa World* and numerous other books. He was a contributing editor of the two southwest volumes of *The Handbook of North American Indians* and coeditor of *Myths and Legends of North American Indians.* Dr. Ortiz has also written dozens of articles for both scholarly and general publications. Among his professional affiliations, he was a MacArthur Foundation Fellow from 1982 to 1987.

Triloki N. Pandey, Professor of Anthropology at the University of California at Santa Cruz, has been working among Native Americans of the Southwest since shortly after arriving in the United States from his native India in 1964. He has focused special attention on the Zuni and other Pueblo peoples, and among his many publications, Dr. Pandey was a contributor to *The Handbook of North American Indians,* Southwest Volume. He is a Fellow of Crown College at the University of California.

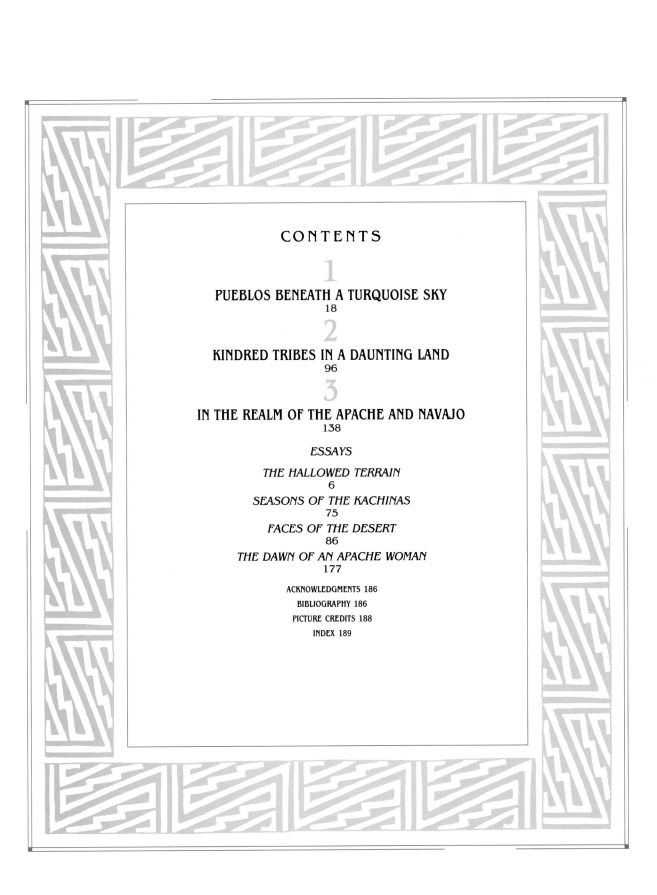

# CONTENTS

*1*

# THE HALLOWED TERRAIN

*Looming over the valley below and the desert beyond, Arizona's snow-clad San Francisco Peaks inspire reverence in several tribes. The Hopi believe that the cloud-swathed range shelters the essential rain spirits. For the Navajo, the peaks mark one of the four corners of their ancestral lands. And the San Carlos Apache say beneficent beings called the mountain spirit people dwell atop the peaks.*

The ties that bind the Indians of the Southwest to their desert homelands are far more complex than mere territorial claims. For the mesas and mountains and canyons and cliffs composing this formidably beautiful region are held sacred by the desert peoples, and veneration of the land is inextricably entwined with a tribe's way of life. Indeed, according to Indian tradition, everything on earth—from sand and rocks to animals and plants to lightning and thunder—is hallowed. Disturbing or failing to honor any part of it is believed to result in tragic disharmony. The Indians believe that their physical and mystical connections to their lands are vital not only to the maintenance of their religious practices but also to their very cultural integrity.

Certain spectacular sites, such as those shown on the following pages, have long been regarded as especially holy by the desert Indians. Some of these landmarks are honored as the abodes of gods or supernatural spirits. Others are revered as the loci of creation, points where the first people of a tribe emerged onto earth. Ancestral legends imbue some landscapes with healing powers. And frequently a sacred place is also a source of water, the literal life-giver in the arid world of the desert.

*The evening sun casts its radiance on Baboquivari Peak in south-central Arizona, venerated by Papago (Tohono O'odham) and Pima Indians as the physical and spiritual center of their universe. Papago legend attests the stunning sunsets were a gift from their creator, Elder Brother, the spirit of goodness who watches over the people from his home on the stony slope.*

*An oasis in the midst of the sun-baked Grand Canyon, Havasu Canyon has been inhabited and honored by the Havasupai Indians for countless centuries. The Havasupai, whose name translates as "people of the blue-green water," believe the springs that feed the canyon's creek and falls possess curative powers.*

Crowned by white granite bluffs, Spirit Mountain in southern Nevada is holy to the Mohave and the Hualapai, as well as to all other Indian peoples whose language traces to the Yuman tongue. These so-called Yuman tribes regard the rugged peak as the portal through which human life emerged after the world had been ravaged by a great flood.

A sandstone spire jutting 800 feet above the floor of Arizona's Canyon de Chelly, Spider Rock—the formation at near left—is honored by the Hopi and Navajo as the lair of the earth goddess Spider Woman. According to Hopi legend, Spider Woman serves as a powerful link between the human world and the world of the divine. The Navajo invoke her name to discipline unruly children.

Awash with the golden glow of sunrise, sheer cliffs in the Grand Canyon—sacred to the Hopi—soar thousands of feet above the Colorado River at their base. Somewhere at the bottom of the majestic canyon, say the Hopi, is the original sipapu—the hole from which humans emerged from the underworld to live on earth.

*From caves high atop Texas's Guadalupe Peak—the summit at far left—the first mountain spirit dancers entered the world, according to the Mescalero Apache. Considered a conduit to heavenly power, the beings are impersonated by masked performers in the Mountain Spirit Dance, an age-old Apache ritual used to cure illness, banish bad fortune, and usher a girl into maturity.*

*Rising like an island from the sandy bottom of the New Mexico desert, Katzimo, or Enchanted Mesa, has long been revered by the Acoma Indians as the site of their ancestral pueblo. According to legend, most of the tribe was tending crops in the valley below when a savage storm swept away the stone steps to the 400-foot mesa, stranding a few doomed souls at its top and forcing the tribe's relocation.*

1

# PUEBLOS BENEATH A TURQUOISE SKY

*Water jug delicately balanced on her head, a woman of Cochiti Pueblo in north-central New Mexico wears a Spanish-style mantilla and traditional bootlike moccasins in this 1920 photograph. Cochiti, like other eastern pueblos once ruled by Spain, has long followed a combination of Spanish and Indian customs.*

In the irrigated fields around Santo Domingo Pueblo, the corn is fast maturing by early August, nourished by the waters of the Rio Grande and the sunlight drunk from the vast New Mexico sky. Seeds planted carefully in April have sent roots deep into the soil, and in late September or early October, if all goes well, the stalks will be laden with kernel-crowded ears—more than enough to feed the community. But for the people of Santo Domingo, as for Pueblo Indians everywhere, corn is not just food. Given to them long ago by the female deity Iyatiko, whose heart is corn and who waits beside a portal through which all mortals must pass when their lives end, the plant has sacred significance, symbolizing the bonds between humankind and the spirit world. In this pueblo, August 4 is a day for prayerful dancing to honor the hidden powers of earth and sky—powers that not only protect and ripen the corn but sustain the entire structure of human existence.

The scene has anomalous notes. As with all the Pueblo communities of the Southwest, the life of this community is a product of both Euro-American and native inheritances. The 2,000 or so Santo Domingo Indians, like other Pueblo peoples, speak English in addition to a language of their own. Many of their one- or two-story adobe homes have electricity and running water. Modern roads run across the 75,000 acres of reservation land, linking the community to the wider world, including a Spanish-founded city, Santa Fe, lying only about 35 miles to the northeast. Spain gave these sedentary southwestern peoples their only collective name: *Pueblo* means "town" in Spanish.

In religion, too, cultural mixing is evident. Just outside the pueblo is a Roman Catholic mission church, and mere hours before the Indians begin the Corn Dance in the plaza on August 4, they attend Mass to celebrate the feast day of Saint Dominic, their town's patron saint. But the new religion and the older beliefs coexist easily, without competing. Mass will be followed by a ceremony that transports the community into a purely

*The Southwest is home to a diverse array of tribes, each with a distinctive culture but all well adapted to survival in the often-challenging, arid landscapes of the region. This map shows generalized boundaries and locations at the earliest point for which there is accurate informa- tion for each tribe—a period ranging from the 16th to the 18th centuries and roughly corresponding to the times of extensive European contact with each group.*

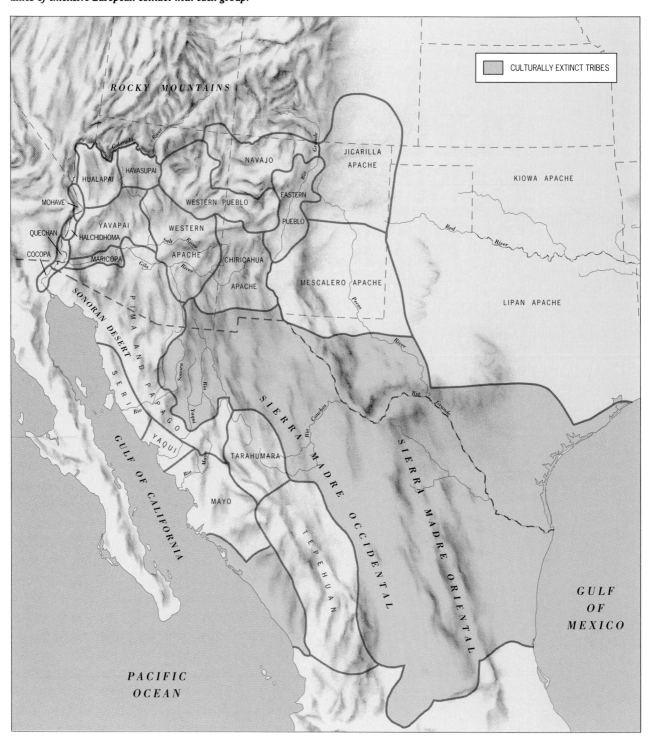

CULTURALLY EXTINCT TRIBES

ROCKY MOUNTAINS

Colorado River

HUALAPAI

HAVASUPAI

NAVAJO

JICARILLA APACHE

KIOWA APACHE

MOHAVE

WESTERN PUEBLO

EASTERN

Rio Grande

QUECHAN

YAVAPAI

WESTERN

PUEBLO

HALCHIDHOMA

Salt River

COCOPA

MARICOPA

Gila River

APACHE

CHIRICAHUA

Red River

APACHE

MESCALERO APACHE

Pecos

LIPAN APACHE

SONORAN DESERT

PIMA AND PAPAGO

River

SERI

Rio Sonora

Rio Yaqui

YAQUI

Rio

SIERRA MADRE OCCIDENTAL

Rio Conchos

Rio Grande

SIERRA MADRE ORIENTAL

Rio Mayo

TARAHUMARA

GULF OF CALIFORNIA

MAYO

TEPEHUAN

GULF OF MEXICO

PACIFIC OCEAN

Indian world, ancient, intricate, and in many ways as vital as it ever was.

In a public dance, the Pueblo sense of the sacred—frequently kept hidden from outside eyes, or revealed in only the most general terms—shows itself with extraordinary vividness. The Santo Domingo Corn Dance gets under way as figures called Koshare pour forth from one of the town's two kivas, ceremonial chambers where the performers have spent weeks practicing and preparing for this day. The Koshare are clowns of a sort—irrepressible, unpredictable, mocking, sometimes gluttonous or obscene as they express the primordial energy of the cosmos. They represent ancestral spirits from the subterranean world, and their supposed origin in the land of the dead is indicated by whitened faces, black and white body paint, and clothing that includes dry cornhusks and rabbit skins. One of their roles during the Corn Dance is to provide protection to the living. In an elaborate historical pantomime, they send runners out from the pueblo to scan the countryside for enemies; the actor-runners return with news of approaching Apache, Navajo, Ute, or Comanche raiders—nomads who, in times gone by, preyed on the Pueblo peoples as crops matured. Amid much excitement, the pantomime continues with a purification ceremony that readies Santo Domingo's own warriors for battle and ensures that they will be victorious in the imaginary clash. With this ritual response to danger, the historical portion of the drama ends. Now comes the central matter: the dancing to guarantee the growth of the precious corn itself.

Members of the audience watch the long ceremonial wands atop the roofs of Santo Domingo's two kivas. The wands are laden with emblems of the natural world. At the peak of each pole are brilliantly colored parrot and woodpecker feathers; a fox skin hangs below; and along the length of the pole is a banner edged with eagle feathers and decorated with symbols of clouds and rain. The removal of a wand from a kiva roof by a rain priest signals that the dancing is about to start. From the kiva issues a multitude of dancers—equal numbers of men and women. They follow the wand-carrying priest into the plaza. With the group comes a chorus of men and a drummer holding a large, double-headed instrument. Drumbeats and chanting will provide the accompaniment to the dance, weaving a musical fabric of subtle, ever-shifting, hypnotic rhythms.

Until sunset, two groups of dancers—one from each kiva in the pueblo—will perform alternately in the plaza. Dressed in traditional costume, with their hair hanging loose, they pay mimetic homage to the powers of nature. The men wear feathers in their hair as symbols of the sky and

*Hopi parents traditionally give simple wooden kachina dolls to their offspring as their first toys. Usually hung on or near the baby's cradle to bring the child good health, the doll represents the deity Hahay'iwuuti, or "mother kachina," who embodies all of the qualities of a good mother.*

clouds. At their throats are shell necklaces, and behind their knees are turtle rattles or bells; in the movements of the dance, these articles evoke the sound of rain on corn plants. The men hold branches of evergreen spruce or fir, representing fertility and longevity. Their kilts and sashes are adorned with sacred signs, and their moccasins are trimmed with skunk fur to fend off evil spirits.

The female dancers are barefoot, affirming the close links of woman-kind to Mother Earth. On their heads are thin, turquoise boards, called

*Sacred Koshare clowns of San Juan Pueblo, popularly known as Black Eyes because of the painted circles on their faces, strike comic poses during a tribal ceremony. The antics of the clowns inject a welcome note of humor into the most solemn of rituals.*

tablitas, that display painted or carved images of the sun, the moon, the arch of the heavens, or other sky motifs. Wisps of eagle down, symbolizing the rain-bearing clouds, are attached to the boards or to the dancers' hair. Each woman wears a one-piece black dress fastened at the right shoulder, and around her waist is a woven belt, red, green, or black in color—all sacred hues. Necklaces, rings, and bracelets abound.

As each dancing group takes its turn in the plaza, men and women form two facing lines and begin to stamp and shuffle their feet to the rhythms of drum and chant. For a time, the sexes continue to dance in separate lines, with the entire group turning about from time to time. Then couples form, and each man dances in a high-stepping style in front of his female partner, who moves at a slower, gentler pace, her eyes cast down. As darkness approaches, the two groups join in a final spectacular dance beseeching divine aid and protection. At last, drum and chorus fall silent. Out in the fields, the corn plants gleam in the twilight, emblematic of the goodness of the earth.

The Corn Dance is just one of many yearly ceremonies that maintain Santo Domingo's place in the scheme of the universe. Not all pueblos are so conscientious about performing traditional rites, but—if only in secret, or mostly among the elders—the pulse of

*A clown hunter holds the rickety bow he will use to shoot harmless sticks at the performers during San Juan's Deer Dance.*

spirituality beats strong almost everywhere. That pulse has never flagged. The spiritual dimension of Pueblo life accounts for the sturdiness of much else in their culture. What the Pueblos believe and how they live have not pulled apart under the pressure of modernity. In a very real sense, the spirit beings worshiped by the Pueblos continue to fulfill their primordial role—preserving those who honor them.

Unity has never been part of Pueblo strength. In Spanish times, their communities were several times as numerous as they are today, but all have been autonomous throughout their histories. Even in speech, the Pueblos are highly fragmented: Four distinct linguistic families spawned their languages, often with dialects that have drifted apart. The Hopi, living in the semidesert of northeastern Arizona, speak a version of the Uto-Aztecan linguistic family, shared by non-Pueblo peoples as diverse as the

*In this 1935 photograph, dancers descend the kiva steps of San Ildefonso Pueblo, enacting the ritual of the Butterfly Dance, a ceremony*

*celebrating youth, fertility, and the beauty of the natural world.*

Ute of Colorado and the Aztecs of Mexico; Hopi villages just a few miles apart have subtly different modes of speech. A completely different language is spoken by the Zuni, living just across the border in New Mexico; their tongue may be related to a California language family called Penutian. Beyond the Zuni in New Mexico, extending from arid country into the valley of the Rio Grande, are communities speaking versions of the Keresan language, unrelated to any other known linguistic stock of American Indians; Santo Domingo, on the east bank of the Rio Grande, is a Keresan pueblo. All the remaining Pueblo peoples living along the same river or its tributaries derive their languages from a family called Tanoan. Three distinct Tanoan tongues are spoken: Tiwa, Tewa, and Towa.

In addition to linguistic distinctions, Pueblo populations separate into two broad cultural subgroups, generally called Western and Eastern but sometimes termed Desert and River. The Western contingent consists of the Hopi, the Zuni, and a pair of Keresan-speaking communities, Acoma and Laguna. Their mode of social organization is clan-based, emphasizing maternal lineage. Among most of the Eastern Pueblos, by contrast, a dualistic organization predominates, with communities divided into halves (moieties in scholarly parlance) and numerous social responsibilities parceled out accordingly. Western and Eastern Pueblo Indians differ also in modes of governance, in their dealings with supernatural powers, and in many other ways. Yet all the far-scattered communities belong unmistakably to a single remarkable culture.

The economic basis of that culture is farming. Several thousand years ago, the secret of growing corn spread into this region from Middle America, and by the middle of the first millennium AD, the ancestors of the Pueblos had developed improved versions of the corn plant—strains that were far more productive than the first domesticated grasses, well suited to the difficult growing conditions of the Southwest, and possessing such special virtues as ease of grinding or good storage qualities. The Indians also grew beans, squash, and some cotton from the time of their early settlements, and when the Spaniards arrived in the area in the 16th century, the Pueblo peoples broadened their agricultural scope to include such new crops as wheat, oats, onions, chilies, peas, melons, and peaches. The Spaniards also introduced a number of domesticated animals—cattle, horses, burros, and, most important, sheep (wool soon replaced cotton as the favored material of Indian weavers).

But wild nature was also an indissoluble part of the Pueblo way of life. The Indians' knowledge of plants was enormous: They gathered dozens of kinds of roots, leaves, berries, nuts, seeds, and fungi. In September, the cones of the piñon tree began to fall and spill nuts on the ground, and families camped in the uplands for weeks at a time to collect the nuts by the basketful. The wild onion was either eaten raw or added to a meat stew. The fruit of the prickly pear cactus supplied valuable nutrition during the months before the corn ripened. The fruit of the broad-leaved yucca provided a sweetener. The yucca's roots yielded a kind of soap—still important in Pueblo rituals, producing lather that symbolizes clouds—and its leaves were a source of fibers to make cord and rope. The leaves and roots of a large number of other plants were used for curative purposes, and the woody parts of almost every bush and tree seemed to serve a purpose: willow and sumac stems for basketry; the wood of the chokecherry for bows; the mountain mahogany for clubs.

*Villagers of Santa Clara Pueblo perform the Green Corn Dance, a ritual that was enacted during the spring and summer months in order to ensure the propagation of corn, the basis of pueblo life. The ceremony beseeches the spirits for rain, a bountiful harvest, and the well-being of the community.*

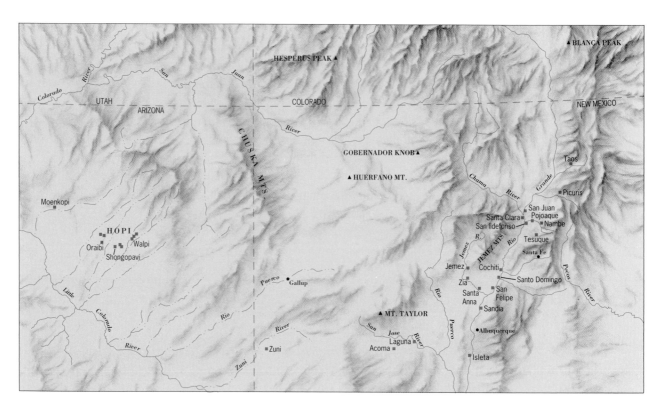

Although the Indians mostly ate vegetable foods, they were skillful hunters. Near home, small creatures were the principal game—ground squirrels, gophers, and especially rabbits. But Pueblo men also traveled far afield in search of antelope, deer, mountain sheep, and other large mammals. Eastern communities regularly sent hunters out into the immensity of the Great Plains for buffalo, but even the Hopi and the Zuni, living far from the grasslands, went after buffalo at times. A big game hunt was a communal enterprise and usually involved a drive—forcing the animals into a canyon, a makeshift corral, or perhaps deep snow, then shooting them with bow and arrow. Rabbits, too, were hunted by the drive method: Hunters formed a slowly closing circle and felled their leaping prey with throwing sticks.

Animals were naturally valued for their meat, but their usefulness extended into many phases of domestic and ceremonial life as well. Drums and articles of clothing were made from their hides, tools from their bones, bowstrings from their sinews, and rattles from their hoofs. The women of one Tewa-speaking community typically offered this prayer when their husbands set off across the grasslands: "Buffalo hides he shall

*Spread out across a portion of the sun-baked lands of their ancestors, the Pueblo peoples today are divided into two main groups based in part on location. The Tanoan- and Keresan-speaking Eastern Pueblos are concentrated along the Rio Grande and its tributaries; the others—Hopi, Zuni, Acoma, and Laguna—occupy the less well watered expanses to the west.*

*These wooden gaming tubes were used in a gambling game once played by Hopi men and women inside the kiva. The object of the game was to guess under which tube a small ball or stone was hidden. The games were typically played in January to relieve the monotony of the long winter vigils between religious ceremonies.*

find for me; costly things he shall find for me."
Still, to a degree rare on the North American continent, the Pueblos were sedentary, firmly fastened to the earth. Their way of life was rooted in earlier southwestern cultures: the Hohokam, who had lived along the Gila and Salt rivers in south-central Arizona; the Mogollon, who dwelt in simple villages in the rugged highlands south of modern Pueblo country; and the Anasazi, whose culture was centered on the Four Corners region of the Southwest—the area around the intersection of Utah, Colorado, Arizona, and New Mexico—until drought, deforestation, and overcultivation of their fields probably drove them south to settle among other groups.

Many features of these ancient cultures were incorporated into the Pueblo lifestyle. Like the Hohokam, builders of an immense network of canals that enabled them to open up arid lands for farming, the Pueblos mastered the techniques of irrigation, drawing on the Rio Grande along a hundred miles of its length and tapping its small and less reliable tributaries as well. Like the Mogollon, who lived in semisubterranean pit houses and were highly accomplished in the arts of pottery, the Pueblos carved some of their rooms out of the earth, and they too were gifted potters. Like the Anasazi, who concentrated their population in multilevel, apartment-style complexes, the Pueblos built boldly upward, stacking their rooms several stories high around a central courtyard. The array of languages spoken by the Pueblos suggests the impact of other influences reaching their communities from farther afield—from tribes of the Great Basin and the Rocky Mountain areas, and from the nomadic tribes who followed the buffalo herds across the Great Plains and structured their lives around hunting and warfare.

But the Pueblo blending of all these cultures was unique. When they built underground, it was for religious motives rather than as a simple way to

*Wearing war paint and war bonnets in the style of Comanche warriors, the men of San Ildefonso Pueblo begin the yearly Comanche Dance commemorating long-ago battles with that fierce Plains Indian tribe. All the Eastern Pueblos stage the event, which is social rather than religious in nature.*

wall out the elements. When they fought wars, it was generally for defensive reasons rather than to gain plunder or fulfill the requisites of manhood. When they founded a new village, the site was typically out in the open, in contrast to the Anasazi habit of seeking the protection of rock overhangs and other secure locations. Still, with their strong walls and absence of ground-level openings, the villages presented a severe challenge to any would-be enemies. The only way into them was by ladder, and access could thus be easily denied in moments of threat.

The villages generally held about 200 people, and their design offered an efficient scheme for domestic life. Rooms were built up in tiers, with each successive tier set back so that the roofs of rooms below served as balconies for those above. On the balconies, families stacked firewood, dried their harvested crops, and worked at various domestic tasks—weaving, making pottery, even cooking—when the weather was good. At night and in less clement weather, life moved indoors. When the cold winter winds began to blow, the upper rooms might be abandoned altogether, with families descending into the dark spaces on lower levels, which were also used for storage.

Each family occupied a single room, about 12 feet by 14 feet in its horizontal dimensions, and entered by means of a ladder extended through a hatchway in the roof. To make the most of the scanty light coming from a fire or through the hatchway, the walls of the room were sometimes whitewashed with gypsum—pounded, baked, ground fine, and moistened before application. Furnishings were minimal. A masonry bench ran along two walls and provided a shelf or a place to sit. Some niches in the walls served as cupboards, but dishes and cooking utensils were mostly kept on the floor. There were no chairs: The elderly sometimes sat on blocks of wood, but most people used folded blankets for seating. At night, they wrapped themselves in the same blankets, perhaps added some furs for warmth, and slept in a row.

Although many days were enlivened by games or set aside for dances and other ceremonial performances, daily life involved plenty of work. The men were mostly out in the fields, sometimes located miles away, and the day would begin with a run to reach them. The women carried water, tended small gardens, looked after the children, and handled a range of food-related jobs. The weeks after the harvest were especially busy. After the men had brought the corn into the village and the ears had been dried on the roofs, the women attended to storage; as cold weather settled in, they sorted through the ears, threw away any that had grown

# A HOMEPLACE AWASH IN THE SUN

At first glimpse, the remarkable pueblo of Zuni has elicited wonder from outsiders, including a 19th-century visitor who described the place as a "gigantic mud honeycomb." But in the minds of the Zuni people, this village and others in western New Mexico were perfect adaptations to a harsh environment, a sedentary farming life, and a culture rich in ceremony. While neighboring nomads ranged across the Southwest in search of food and plunder, the Zuni developed permanent settlements that best met the practical and spiritual needs of their close-knit community.

The heart of a Zuni town was the central plaza, where public rituals were held and around which the first dwellings were erected. The living quarters generally faced south to catch maximum sunlight during the cold-weather months. Built of stone and adobe, the thick walls of these structures absorbed heat during the day and released it slowly, keeping the rooms warm during frigid winter nights. Stories were added in tiers, creating terraces that caught the sun and provided a view of the plaza. The Zuni used the terraces as workspaces; there they baked bread in conic ovens and hung out strings of vegetables to dry.

For defensive purposes, ground floors had no external doors, and entry to the pueblos, according to the Zuni expression, was accomplished by going "up the ladder and down the ladder." Inside, furnishings were minimal, amounting to little more than clay pots, baskets, sleeping blankets, and grinding stones. Most rooms were set aside for sleeping and food preparation, while darker rooms deep within the complex held stores of food.

A cross section of a Zuni pueblo shows its division into food storage space; terraces overlooking the plaza; and living rooms, where one woman grinds corn, another tends to a child, and a third stokes a fire. Ladders provided access to the rooms, as shown in the photograph taken in 1903 by Edward Curtis (inset).

moldy, and redried others. When beans were picked, men broke the pods open by threshing them with a stick; the women then tossed pods and beans in a basket tray to let the wind separate them. The ripening of the pumpkins brought still other duties: The women cut the rind off with a knife, sliced the pumpkins in half, and hung the pieces out in the sun to dry; each half was cut into a spiral strip, which was fully dried for storage.

A variety of methods were used in the preparation of meals. Beans were usually boiled, as were pumpkins and squash. Corn could be boiled or roasted after the harvest, when it was still fresh. But the starting point for most corn-based dishes was flour. On most days, Pueblo women spent several hours grinding a fresh batch of the cornmeal. It was a sequential process: Dried kernels were stripped from an ear, placed on a

*A modern Hopi girl wears her hair in the squash-blossom style, a traditional fashion for maidens of marriageable age, now displayed only for ceremonies. At left, a woman creates the style: After parting the girl's hair in the middle, she forms the whorls by winding the hair in a figure eight pattern around a frame of bent willow.*

rough-textured stone, and laboriously rubbed with a smaller stone; then, as the kernels broke down, the particles were moved to a series of progressively smoother stones to reduce them to the desired fine texture. So fundamental was cornmeal to the diet of the Pueblos that, before marriage, a Hopi girl had to spend four days grinding in the household of her betrothed to show that she was qualified to be his wife.

The flour yielded a wide range of dishes—30 or more. It might be put into boiling water to produce a gruel, and it was transformed into many sorts of dumplings and breads. A favorite bread was a wafer variety, made by spreading a cornmeal batter on a smooth, flat stone that had been heated for hours. But not every dish required flour. Sometimes the corn kernels were soaked in a solution of wood ashes; the shells fell off, and the starchy interior swelled. The swollen kernels, called hominy, could be ground up and made into pancakes. After the Spaniards came, these pancakes would be known as tortillas.

In a sense, the Spaniards were eager to meet the Pueblos—but only because they were laboring under a great misconception. Spanish explorers entered the American Southwest in 1539, drawn north from Mexico by rumors of cities glinting with gold and gems—possibly the Seven Cities of Cíbola, which, according to legend, had been established somewhere far to the west of Europe by Catholic bishops fleeing Muslims. The trail of rumor led to the Zuni, then living in six villages along a tributary of the Little Colorado River in present-day New Mexico. A Franciscan missionary with the exploration party described the hopeful approach: "We came in sight of Cíbola, which lies in a plain on the slope of a round height. Its appearance is very good for settlement, the handsomest I have seen in these parts." Later, giving full vent to his imagination, he told of seeing a town "larger than the city of Mexico," big enough to "encompass two Sevilles." The houses, he said, were inlaid with turquoise.

Unfortunately for the newcomers' dreams of wealth, the Zuni proved militant and drove the Spaniards off without much difficulty. But the Pueblo world had been breached, and it would never be the same. The following year, the conquistador Francisco Vásquez de Coronado arrived

*Sitting beneath a row of chilies hung up to dry, a Towa woman husks corn in the plaza of Jemez Pueblo in 1936. The Indians separate the corn by color: blue corn for cornmeal, white for ceremonial purposes, and mixed yellow and red for cattle feed. The best ears of each type are reserved for seed.*

*A Pueblo woman bakes corn bread in an oven called a "horno," the traditional outdoor cooking place still used in villages in the Southwest. Introduced by the Spaniards, the beehive-shaped structures are fired with wood.*

with a large military force, took over the Zuni village of Hawikuh as a base, and spent a year and a half investigating the area and its Indian inhabitants. "Cíbola" and the country around it proved a grave disappointment in terms of riches, but Coronado was impressed in other ways. He located scores of towns housing tens of thousands of people, an echo—on a smaller scale—of agriculture-based Indian civilizations in Middle America. Although the towns looked nothing like the temple-centered cities of Mexico, their apartment-style architecture exerted its own fascination. The newcomers commented on the defensive virtues of the walled, doorless pueblos and their dense, modular construction. And they were struck by how the towns seemed to grow out of the earth.

The pueblos in the west were frequently built with slabs of sandstone, the soft yellow or reddish rock quarried from the sides of mesas. The sandstone was split into blocks, layered to erect walls, chinked with small stones, and plastered with mud. Towns in the east were constructed primarily of adobe, a material created by mixing the two components on which Pueblo existence was founded: earth and water. The recipe called for clay to be blended with sand or straw to give it strength and to prevent cracking when it dried. Originally, adobe walls were made by supporting the wetted mixture with poles or adding stones as an internal reinforcement and building the wall handful by handful. Adobe bricks came into use after the arrival of the Spaniards. When the bricks had been laid, the walls were covered with a wash of adobe plaster to seal joints and give them a smooth, clean appearance.

At least outwardly, the Spaniards brought many changes to the Pueblo world, but particularly along the Rio Grande, the most populous and productive area. The first significant colonizing effort was led by Juan de Oñate, who marched into the region in 1598 at the head of a party of 400 soldiers and settlers. The expedition came equipped with seed, livestock, household goods, and iron tools—whatever the Spaniards needed to take root on this northernmost frontier of their New World domain. Prior tenancy was hardly a consideration. Oñate claimed immense tracts of territory along the Rio Grande, explaining to Pueblo leaders that the power of Spain would henceforth protect the Indians from their enemies. In return, he expected the Pueblos to acknowledge the supreme authority of King Philip II of Spain and also to surrender their own religion in favor of Christianity. To baptize them and provide the necessary religious guidance, he had brought along 10 Franciscans, eight friars and two lay brothers.

Oñate was a poor leader, dissipating his energies on a variety of get-rich-quick schemes and paying little attention to the activities of either the settlers or the missionaries. After about a decade, he was replaced, and the drive to impose Spanish ways on the land gained new impetus. Santa Fe was founded in the winter of 1609-1610 and thereafter served as the center of colonizing efforts. More missionaries arrived, establishing an administrative headquarters in the pueblo they named Santo Domingo and building other missions throughout the Rio Grande Valley. According to their own reports, they enjoyed spectacular success in the harvesting of Indian souls. By 1625, they said, more than 30,000 Indians had been baptized in 28 pueblos. Some of their claims of conversions ranged up to the half-million mark—estimates worthy of the Franciscan who, a century earlier, had described the glories of Cíbola.

The missionaries worked to convert the local peoples in the secular sphere as well as the spiritual. They introduced the Pueblos to livestock, new crops, and metal tools, impressing them with the material potency of the European way of life—and no doubt enhancing the receptiveness of many Indians to their religious ideas, since these would presumably be potent as well. In certain respects, the newcomers' religion was not entirely alien. Just as the Spaniards worshiped in a church, the Pueblos had a sacred place for ritual: the kiva. Religious observance in both traditions involved altars, chants, a sacred calendar, and sacred utensils. Ceremonial tobacco smoke was a kind of parallel to incense. Catholic holy water was reminiscent of the water that Indian priests used in rain ceremonies.

But the differences of the two religious traditions were far more numerous and fundamental than the similarities. Indian belief in a multitude of spirit beings was thoroughly incompatible with Catholic monotheism.

The Indians had nothing resembling the Catholic notions of heaven and hell; they believed that all people, regardless of merit, went to the same afterworld, where they lived much as they had on earth. The Indians also had no version of the Christian ideas of atonement and redemption. They even saw the earth differently. The Indians sought harmony with the earth, whereas the Europeans saw it as a source of wealth.

The missionaries were not interested in bridging the gap. They viewed Pueblo religious beliefs as barbaric and benighted. Few missionaries bothered to learn Indian languages and thus gain some comprehension of native culture. In much the same spirit, they rarely took the trouble to teach the Indians to read and write Spanish; what education they did offer tended to be perfunctory, superficial, and by dictum. They imposed their own views of morality on the Indian population without the slightest regard for ancient custom. Among the Pueblos, for example, divorce was commonplace and straightforward: The husband or wife simply moved out of the house, and any children stayed where they were. To the missionaries, this practice was sinful, symptomatic of what they saw as promiscuity in Indian culture. They forbade it.

Many of the Pueblos were willing to add Christian sacraments and rituals to their own forms of worship, seeing the mix as cumulative rather than incongruous. But the missionaries rejected any possibility of the two traditions coexisting. The old beliefs had to be eradicated, and they were entirely prepared to take strong measures to achieve that end. They seized kivas and sealed them off. They burned sacred masks and other ceremonial equipment. They prohibited dancing in the pueblo plazas. Meanwhile, they permitted no backsliding among the baptized: Anyone who did not attend Mass each day was punished.

Inevitably, these heavy-handed tactics touched off explosions. In 1639 the Taos Indians killed the resident priest and destroyed the church that had been built at their pueblo. During the next decade, residents of several pueblos demonstrated against the flogging and jailing of Indians who had secretly continued the old forms of worship. The Spanish authorities hanged 29 of the leaders of this protest movement.

The assault on their religion was only one of many hardships suffered by the Indians. Colonists were pouring into the area, establishing ranches and farms all along the Rio Grande. They not only settled on Pueblo lands but also demanded a tribute of food, labor, and material goods. Between 1667 and 1672, drought decimated the crops. In 1671 epidemic disease swept across the land. Then—in spite of all the reassuring Spanish words about protecting the Rio Grande peoples from their enemies—Apache and Navajo warriors, more potent than ever because of their acquisition of horses, descended on the Indian villages in a series of devastating raids. By 1680 the beleaguered Pueblos had reached the point of desperation. Suspending ancient habits of independence, communities all across the Southwest joined together in an attempt to reclaim their land by force. The uprising succeeded at first: The Spaniards were driven out and did not return for 12 years.

But nothing was solved. Droughts continued to weaken the Pueblos; Indian enemies continued to harry them; and the concerted action that had made victory possible soon lapsed into bitter factionalism. By the time Spanish rule was reestablished by a returning army in 1692, the overall Pueblo population had been reduced to perhaps a quarter of its original level, and many communities stood abandoned. There were no

*Zuni war god effigies guard the entrance to a tribal shrine on Twin Mountain in New Mexico. Important deities in past centuries when the Zuni had to battle the Apache and other hostile tribes, the war gods are still worshiped at a special ceremony each year. The effigies are traditionally carved of wood from trees that have been split by lightning.*

*This Zuni prayer bowl is designed to hold the mixture of cornmeal and turquoise that is sprinkled on ritual items during rain ceremonies. The bowl's stepped corners represent the four cardinal directions; the frog and tadpole decorations are symbols of fertility.*

more rebellions of any significance—in part because the Spaniards took steps to keep the peace: The Indians were given royal title to their lands, and the Franciscan missionaries were never again allowed to resume their coercive proselytizing.

The Southwest would see further political upheavals, but with the Pueblos usually in the role of bystanders. In 1821 Mexico declared its independence from Spain, a shift that hardly affected the Pueblos, although the Mexican government was often lax about preventing white encroachment on the Indians' lands. In 1846 the United States went to war against Mexico and swiftly won possession of the Southwest. Encroachment by settlers worsened for a time, but gradually the land grabbing diminished, and the Indians' hold on their physical place in the world firmed.

Meanwhile, the Pueblos—unlike many other Native Americans—had found a kind of cultural stability. From Spanish times forward, they sustained their lifestyle by a balancing act. They took what they wanted of

*A Matachine dancer of Santa Clara Pueblo, wearing a conic hat resembling a Catholic bishop's miter, performs with drummers during a ceremony celebrating the expulsion of the Spaniards from Indian territory. The dance, enacted at Christmastime, parallels a similar Spanish dance commemorating the victory of Spain over the Moors.*

non-Indian culture and technology, yet retained their own languages, their own social structures, and—as a basis for all else—their own religion. To the present day, religion remains the bedrock of Pueblo identity.

At the heart of their belief is a view of humans, spirit beings, and nature as bound together into a single whole. According to the Pueblos, spirit beings are a part of the natural world, present in it rather than residing in some separate and superior realm. From the sun deity come gifts of warmth and light that support all living creatures: The Tewa-speaking Pueblos say that the sun passes through a lake after it sets in the west, then travels all night through the underworld to rise again in the east; they describe this source of blessings as a god clothed in white deerskin and hiding his beautiful face behind a mask.

All Pueblos regard certain mountains as sacred, home to deities whose powers often include the genesis of weather. Tewa peoples say that the wind comes from the mountain known as Sandia, where Old Woman Wind is believed to live. The Keresan-speaking people of Acoma Pueblo associate surrounding mountains with gods that bring different varieties of moisture: rain, drizzle, mist, and snow. These mountains are not abstract points in space; they are stitched into the fabric of Pueblo life. In the words of Alfonso Ortiz, a prominent student of his own Tewa culture: "It's impossible to think of people here without thinking of a particular mountain that they have a special relationship with. They look to it for all sorts of things: portents of the weather immediately ahead, signs for the kind of winter they will have; they look to it for evergreens and eagle feathers, which they use in dances, and for pigments and other materials to be used for their ceremonies. Mountain tobacco from a certain elevation is used to send clouds of smoke up to meet the clouds of the sky as a prayer and appeal for rain."

Spatial orientation is developed to an extraordinary degree in Pueblo religion. Sacred mountains mark the four horizontal directions of the earth—north, west, south, east—and also define the boundaries of a community's place in the world. Closer in, there may be four sacred hills, and, closer still, four shrines. The village itself may have four dance plazas. But this quadripartite division is only part of the cosmic picture. In most cases, Pueblo belief is structured around a total of six cardinal directions, with "above" and "below" added to the four horizontals. Particular directions are associated not only with the supernatural beings but also with plants, animals, and objects that have ritual significance. In addition, directions are linked to colors. In the Zuni scheme of symbolic colors, for example, blue corresponds to north, yellow to west, red to south, white to east, multicolored to above, and black to below.

The Tewa believe that humans once lived in a lower world where the sun shone at night, as pale as the moon. Animals, insects, and plants shared this nether realm, and so did many supernatural beings, collectively known as kachinas. Far back in the past, humans left the underworld, making their way upward through a series of spheres with the help of powerful animals, and finally emerging onto the surface of the present world through an opening in the roof of the last subterranean sphere. Other Pueblos hold similar origination beliefs, but there are varying tradi-

*Two life-size mountain lions, carved out of volcanic rock in prehistoric times, crouch in a clearing enclosed by boulders in northern New Mexico. Worn by wind and weather, the ancient shrine is still visited by Pueblo hunters venerating the spirit of the mountain lion: The sun-bleached deer and elk antlers are offerings they have left behind.*

tions as to the location of the entryway, generally known as *sipapu*. The Tewa believe that sipapu lies in a brackish lake set among sand dunes in south-central Colorado. The Hopi say that the ancestral portal is located in the bottom of the Grand Canyon, and the Keresan peoples variously cite a pit or deep caves to the north as the place of emergence.

According to Pueblo belief, the kachinas taught the newly emerged humans how to farm, hunt, organize their society, and preserve good relations with all the forces of the cosmos. The kachinas then migrated away from sipapu; they could not remain in so sacred a place, although all individuals would return to the portal after death, passing back through it to reach the underworld again.

The emergence legend is key to Pueblo religion. Most kivas feature a small hole in the floor, a representation of sipapu. Normally covered, it is reopened for rites that recall the origins of the People. In addition, public ceremonies sometimes include a ritual remembrance of the dawn time.

Tradition says that one of the most important lessons that the kachinas taught to the ancestral Pueblos was the need for cooperation and harmony in human affairs: Humans were instructed to work together to plant corn, irrigate the fields, hunt, gather firewood, and clean the village. Fundamental values in Pueblo society continue to be conformity, collective effort, and the primacy of the group over the individual. The Pueblos frown on people who hunger for power, set themselves apart from the group, or act in a disruptive fashion. At one time, they regarded such nonconformists as witches and often executed them.

In keeping with the cooperative ethic, Pueblo communities all embrace an array of voluntary societies—organizations that recruit their members from the young people of the village, train them in a body of secret lore, and perform specialized duties. In the past, these societies were charged with coordinating or carrying out a range of activities vital to the functioning of the community—roles that were based on claims of affinity with particular spirits and ritual phenomena. Some societies specialized in the management of hunting, a matter that required much ritual preparation. Others were concerned with phases of the agricultural cycle; they performed ceremonies intended to bring the warmth of spring to the ground in order to prepare it for planting, and later in the year to promote the vigorous growth of the crops. Some dealt with human health: Their members were believed to have the power to cure illnesses, or strange diseases suspected of being caused by witchcraft and requiring elaborate rites to undo the sorcery. The policing of a village was the responsibility of a voluntary society. So was the overseeing of war. Before the Zuni launched a raid of reprisal, leaders of the Bow Society prayed: "To be avenged, we have made up our minds. My children, you shall set your minds to be men. You shall think to provide yourself with good weapons. Then perhaps we shall have the good fortune to get what we wish, cleansing our heart, cleansing our thoughts."

All the work of the voluntary societies was holy, and the sacred knowledge that gave members their powers had to be passed along unaltered to successive generations. The organizations were headed by priests, who generally held the top offices for life. This system of leadership fostered stability and undeviating commitment to the secret canon.

Today, although many of the old roles of the societies have faded, they remain critical to the cohesion of their communities. Through their instruction of new members, their prayers and rites in kivas, and their staging of the public ceremonies, the societies do much to perpetuate the traditional view of the Pueblo peoples' place in a spirit-filled universe.

For all the shared features of their belief system—the emergence story, the strong sense of spatial structure in the cosmos, the stressing of social harmony and group effort—Pueblo communities have each evolved their own ceremonial practices, just as they have followed some divergent paths in social organization and in their conduct of daily life. From the Hopi villages in the western desert to the pueblo of Taos on the edge of the Great Plains, the picture of Pueblo culture is complex, but the picture is rich everywhere—richer, indeed, than any outsider can ever know, since much of it is carefully hidden from view.

The Hopi live in a dozen or so villages on and near three flat-topped heights—known by outsiders as First, Second, and Third mesas—that jut out from the southern escarpment of Arizona's Black Mesa. These rocky promontories lie in view of one another, although First and Third mesas are separated by about 15 miles. The total Hopi holdings of mesas and lowlands, including the outlying settlement of Moenkopi, comprise an area of about 500 square miles, lying entirely within the much larger Navajo reservation.

Most of the villages are sited on the barren heights. One of these settlements, Old Oraibi on Third Mesa, was established around 1100; it may be the oldest continuously inhabited site in the United States (although the pueblo of Acoma also claims the title). Until the mid-13th century, the

Hopi communities were more dispersed, with many of them located on lower ground. But over the next centuries, the People gradually concentrated atop the mesas, especially as raids by the Navajo, Apache, and Ute increased and as the potential threat from the Spaniards grew. Since then, new communities have sprung up from time to time, on both mesa and lowland. On one occasion, the Hopi even allowed Tewa-speaking people to settle in their midst: The village of Hano, also called Tewa Village, was founded on First Mesa by refugees seeking to escape the wrath of the Spaniards after the Pueblo Revolt of 1680.

Of all the Pueblo peoples, the Hopi were least affected by the Spaniards. Coronado visited them, but the Spaniards did not approach Hopi country again for another 40 years. Missionaries were virtually the only whites the Hopi encountered during the Spanish era, and the influence the friars exerted was far weaker here than it was among the Eastern Pueblos. Until recently, the Hopi had little interest in Christianity—an attitude that, in concert with their isolation, would help preserve their traditional culture to an unequaled degree among Native Americans.

Although Spanish colonists detected no promise in their dry, remote land, the Hopi saw nature as bountiful, provided they first sought the favor of the divine ones who rule their universe. Hunting supplied some of their food (rabbit drives are still a regular late-year activity). They also gathered more than 100 wild plants for various domestic purposes. The sheep and cattle introduced by the Spaniards became an important element of their economy. But since earliest times, the Hopi have won most of their living from the soil.

Their farming economy is masterfully adapted to the difficult conditions that prevail in the Southwest. Although rain falls in significant quantities only periodically, the Hopi know exactly how it will flow. They place their fields in the path of the floods that are produced by the downpours, and they build dams to hold the precious liquid and direct its movements. A good portion of the rain is absorbed by sand blown against the base of the mesas; this hidden reservoir will feed springs that trickle throughout the year and will supply a steady flow to underground streams that course invisibly beneath the dry terrain.

In spite of climatic obstacles, the Hopi are able to cultivate a multitude of crops. They raise onions, chilies, and other vegetables in small gardens irrigated with spring water, and they grow some beans and fruits on the mesa tops. The primary arena of farming, however, lies along the generally dry watercourses stretching southward across the plain below

*A 1902 photograph shows a Hopi priest wading in the sacred spring of Mishongnovi Pueblo during the climax of the nine-day-long Flute Ceremony, a rainmaking ritual held in late August on alternate years with the Snake Dance Ceremony. During this part of the ritual, the priest is retrieving three jars containing sacred fetishes.*

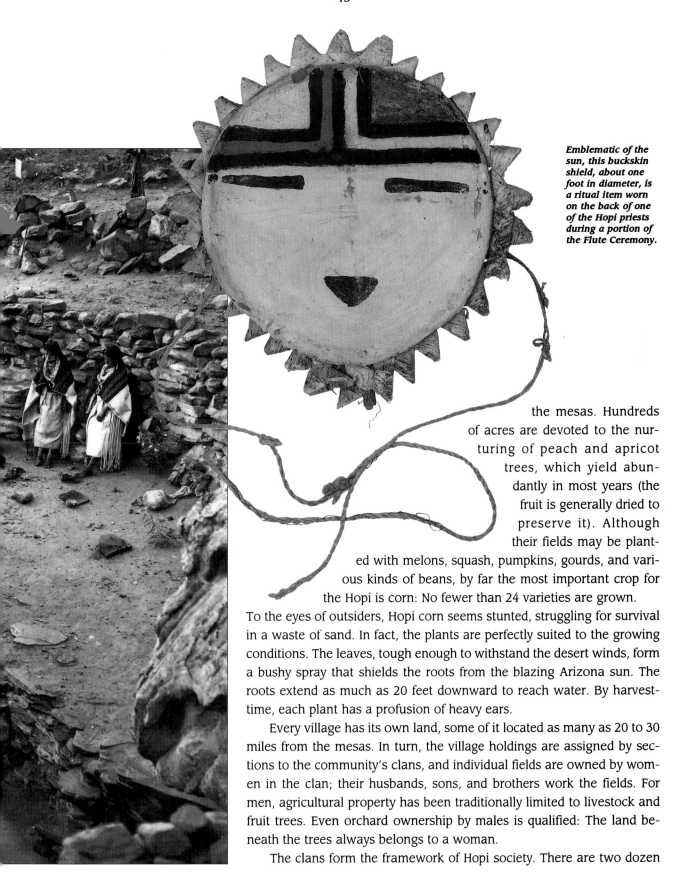

*Emblematic of the sun, this buckskin shield, about one foot in diameter, is a ritual item worn on the back of one of the Hopi priests during a portion of the Flute Ceremony.*

the mesas. Hundreds of acres are devoted to the nurturing of peach and apricot trees, which yield abundantly in most years (the fruit is generally dried to preserve it). Although their fields may be planted with melons, squash, pumpkins, gourds, and various kinds of beans, by far the most important crop for the Hopi is corn: No fewer than 24 varieties are grown.

To the eyes of outsiders, Hopi corn seems stunted, struggling for survival in a waste of sand. In fact, the plants are perfectly suited to the growing conditions. The leaves, tough enough to withstand the desert winds, form a bushy spray that shields the roots from the blazing Arizona sun. The roots extend as much as 20 feet downward to reach water. By harvesttime, each plant has a profusion of heavy ears.

Every village has its own land, some of it located as many as 20 to 30 miles from the mesas. In turn, the village holdings are assigned by sections to the community's clans, and individual fields are owned by women in the clan; their husbands, sons, and brothers work the fields. For men, agricultural property has been traditionally limited to livestock and fruit trees. Even orchard ownership by males is qualified: The land beneath the trees always belongs to a woman.

The clans form the framework of Hopi society. There are two dozen

*Members of a Hopi women's society perform the Lakone Dance in the plaza of their pueblo. Primarily a fertility ceremony, the dance is supposed to bring moisture to the ground in the spring. Popularly called the Basket Dance after the baskets the women carry, the ritual also celebrates the female as the great sustainer of village life.*

or so clans, each of them named for an animal, plant, or some natural or supernatural phenomenon that is seen as an ancestral partner and the source of special powers possessed by the clan members. In the clan scheme, kinship is traced through the mother's line, and marriage within the clan is strictly forbidden. Hopi tradition decrees that when a man gets married, he moves into the household of his wife, which may be shared by a host of other people—her parents and grandparents, sisters and their husbands, and her unmarried brothers. The husband will continue to participate in the activities of his own clan and maintain an association with the homes of his own mother and sisters, but his children will become members of his wife's clan.

The presiding figure of a clan—the Clan Mother—is a matriarch who keeps custody of the group's sacred possessions, prayer sticks, and fetishes. In keeping with tradition, clan members live in houses built next to the matriarch's home. Households that follow the old way of life function as almost-independent economic units. The women prepare the food, carry water up from springs at the foot of the mesa, care for the children, make pottery and baskets, and keep the house in good repair. The men farm, herd livestock, gather wood, and weave.

The matrilineal clans are intimately tied to the ceremonial life of the Hopi villages. Each of the ceremonies conducted during the year is viewed as the property of a particular clan—entrusted to the group by supernatural figures after the Hopi emerged from the underworld. In practice, other clans may play a supporting role, and the actual performance is staged by one or more secret societies, whose members may be drawn from many clans—a system that ensures a distribution of power throughout the village and prevents one clan from gaining a monopoly on some phase of religious observance. Nonetheless, the ownership tie is real: A lineage within the proprietary clan is responsible for the ceremonial equipment, and the head official of the ceremony is a member of that clan (he must also be initiated into the secret society that will carry out the ritual). In addition, the clan is seen as proprietor of the kiva where much of the ceremony takes place.

The number of kivas in each village ranges from two to six. Built either entirely or partly underground, the Hopi chambers are rectangular—in contrast to the circular or oval kivas of most Eastern Pueblos—and oriented north-south where the terrain permits. At times, men come to the kiva to relax, gossip, or discuss issues of importance. But a kiva is also a holy place, and on many days during the year, it is used exclusively for

# THE HOPI'S SACRED CHAMBER

Occupying a mystic realm between the underworld and the world above, the kiva has been at the heart of Pueblo life for more than 1,000 years. Adorned with hand-painted murals that symbolize fertility and rain, these ceremonial chambers are the most holy of sites. For the Hopi and others, they mark the point where life began.

The sipapu is a sacred cavity in the kiva floor that recalls the opening through which the first humans emerged. Leaving their dark home in the earth's interior, they broke through to a realm of dim light and vegetation, represented in the kiva by the main floor. Continuing to climb to a higher plane, humans discovered brighter light and a world of animals—denoted by the kiva's raised platform. And finally, by scaling a great pine tree—the kiva's long-poled ladder—people arrived at the present world.

The Hopi believe they will return to the underworld when they die. Until that time, the sipapu remains their means of communion with the supernatural. Consequently, before emerging from the kiva, ceremonial dancers stomp on the cottonwood plank covering the sipapu, sending prayers echoing down to the spirits below.

Although kivas such as the one above served primarily as ceremonial centers, they were not without their secular uses. At left, a Hopi man sits at a loom suspended from wall beams and secured to a plank in the kiva floor, engaged in the traditionally male craft of blanket weaving.

ceremonial purposes—singing, dancing, smoking (the tobacco smoke is seen as analogous to rain clouds), praying, preparing costumes for public dancing, and erecting altars that bear sacred imagery.

Hopi life is steeped in ritual, composed of an annual succession of ceremonies, great and small, that are seen as essential to the harmonious workings of the universe and maintenance of the safety and health of the community. The ceremonial year divides roughly into halves, with the most intense activity occurring between late December and mid-July. Central to all the rites during these six months are masked performers who become kachinas, the spirit beings who taught the Hopi how to live on earth after the emergence through sipapu, the hole in the roof of the underworld. Perhaps 300 different kachinas may appear in the ceremonies, their masks and paint linking them to particular birds, animals, wild plants, foods, aspects of the weather—all the significant elements of the Hopi world. Only men can wear these masks, and only after careful indoctrination and a lengthy initiation ceremony. The masks are seen as having the power to literally transform the wearer, endowing him with the powers of the spirit being he is impersonating. In this guise, he usually engages in group dances, both in the privacy of the kiva and in the town plaza, but kachinas perform in other ways as well, serving as guards during ceremonies, acting as clowns, and posing as ogres who threaten misbehaving children.

Major ceremonies traditionally begin when the sun rises or sets over a particular landmark, and they may last anywhere from four to 20 days, moving out of the kiva only on the last day or two. The first half of the ceremonial year—the so-called kachina season—is launched at the winter solstice in late December. In a moment of great drama, a single spirit impersonator, called the Soyal kachina, arrives from outside the village and opens the kivas so that other masked dancers may appear. This Hopi New Year is an occasion to ritually strengthen clan houses and seek various sorts of divine favor by depositing offerings at shrines; the offerings—fashioned from smoothed sticks, feathers, string, grass, and other materials, all of symbolic significance—are regarded as prayers in physical form and play a role in most Hopi religious activities.

In the months following the New Year, many more kachinas come to the villages, sometimes bringing gifts for the children—kachina dolls for the girls, ball games or toy bows for the boys. Members of the secret societies spend long periods in the kivas, and the whole village is periodically swept up in public dances to prepare for the time of planting, to take

*Regalia used by a Hopi priest during the Snake Dance, the tribe's most dramatic rainmaking ceremony, include a feathered headdress, a prayer stick carved to resemble a snake, and a decorated kilt. The zigzag pattern on the kilt is representative of both a snake and a lightning bolt; the marks within the zigzag are frog tracks; the colored stripes symbolize a rainbow.*

advantage of the kachinas' rain-bringing gifts, and to promote the fertility of the earth. Finally, in July, comes Niman, a ceremony that celebrates the ripening of the first corn and sends the kachinas back to their underworld home, where they will reside until the time for renewal of the earth comes around again in December.

The ceremonial seeking of nature's blessings continues after the disappearance of the kachinas, although in an entirely different key. Late summer brings ceremonies designed to solicit moisture for the ripening crops. One of these rituals, the Snake Dance, which is performed every other year, honors creatures whose sinuous form is associated with lightning, and hence rain. At the beginning of the Snake Dance ceremony, men of one religious society set out from the village in four directions and spend four days collecting snakes, some of them poisonous. The snake gatherers then join a second society for two days and evenings in a kiva to dramatize mythical events. Subsequently, a race is held, with the winner bringing a gourd of water to the village. Later still, priests dance in the plaza with the writhing snakes in their mouths, while attendants stroke the reptiles to keep them from coiling and striking. At the conclusion of the rite, runners seize the snakes, take them away to sacred locales in the four cardinal directions, and set them free.

As the crops mature in early autumn, Hopi women hold a series of ceremonies in the village plaza, dancing and tossing presents to the onlookers. The children, too, are given the opportunity to perform their own special dances at that time. Then, in late November, young men are initiated into the various religious societies—a fitting conclusion to the ceremonial year, signaling the perpetuation of wisdom that has sustained the Hopi villages since their founding in a distant age.

Across the Arizona-New Mexico border from the Hopi villages live the Zuni, speaking an unrelated language but quite similar in their lifestyle. At the time the Spaniards arrived in the 16th century, the Zuni population was spread among six villages in the valley of the Zuni River, a narrow and erratically flowing tributary of the Little Colorado. Like the Hopi, they resisted conversion by missionaries, and their relations with the intruding power ranged from resentful to violent. In the wake of the great revolt in 1680, they were so apprehensive about Spanish retaliation that they withdrew from their villages and moved to camps on a defensible mesa top, their sacred mountain. A few years later, they returned to their land, but five of the original six pueblos were left abandoned. The entire population congregated in the single village known as Zuni.

*Painted with the markings of their clan, Zuni runners balance kicksticks on their feet, ready to fling them forward and dash in pursuit. Skilled runners could throw the sticks as far as 100 feet while competing in races that stretched for 25 miles. The sticks, shown below in detail, also bore the insignia of the clans.*

Although the Spaniards left them largely alone after the rebellion, the white world began to press closer when the Southwest became American territory. During the years of the gold rush in the mid-19th century, many travelers passed through the area, helping themselves to Zuni livestock and crops. In 1881 the tracks of a transcontinental railroad reached the New Mexico town of Gallup 40 miles to the north, bringing a flood of settlers and traders. Since then, the challenge of keeping their old culture intact has been more difficult for the Zuni than for the isolated Hopi, but they have succeeded to a remarkable extent.

Today the Zuni number about 8,000, approximately the same population as when the Spaniards marched up from Mexico. The majority of

# TALISMANS POTENT WITH POWER

*An alabaster bear fetish is incised with a stylized arrow on its back; the Zuni hold that predators charm their prey with their breath; the arrow, sometimes called a heart line, signifies the pathway of the powerful breath from the lungs to the mouth of the beast.*

Of the pueblo-dwelling Native Americans, the Zuni are particularly recognized for their faith in the power of animal fetishes to assist them in their lives. Contrary to Western conceptions in regard to the superiority of human beings over other living creatures, the Zuni believe that animals—with their keen senses, sharp teeth, claws, talons, stealth, and quickness—are closer to the gods than are people.

A great deal of the meaning behind the animal talismans is known only by members of the secret Zuni medicine societies. According to tribal legend, as the Zuni ancestors emerged from the underworld, the two children of the Zuni supreme being turned many of the most dangerous predators into stone in order to save the people from being devoured. The children allowed the hearts of the animals to continue to live inside the stone, however. It is to the spirits of these predators, captured within the tiny, palm-sized fetishes, that the Zuni turn for assistance. A variety of animal fetishes are available to promote success in diverse personal and communal endeavors, including farming, marital relations, healing the sick, and, especially, the hunting of wild animals.

In keeping with tradition, fetishes are stored inside special earthenware jars where they are fed ceremonial food and water. Some even have offerings of beads or arrowheads tied to them with twine. Should the fetish fail to produce the desired results, it is considered the fault of the owner for not tending it properly, not of the fetish.

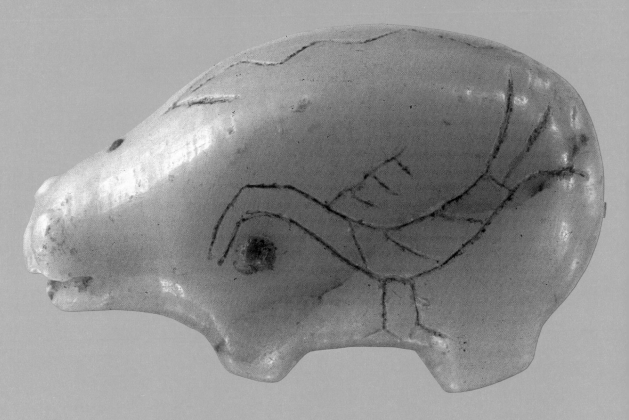

EAGLE—HUNTER GOD OF THE SKY

MOUNTAIN LION—HUNTER GOD OF THE NORTH

COYOTE—HUNTER GOD OF THE WEST

WOLF—HUNTER GOD OF THE EAST

WILDCAT—HUNTER GOD OF THE SOUTH

*These crude, two- to four-inch-long hunting fetishes of the six directions, each of them more than 100 years old, represent the six Zuni hunter gods who rule the game animals of the American Southwest. Zuni men carried such carvings with them in order to ensure a successful hunt. Their choice of a talisman depended on their intended quarry. A mountain lion fetish was preferred for hunting buffalo, elk, and deer; a coyote for mountain sheep; a wildcat or wolf for antelope; and an eagle for rabbit. The mole fetish was used to hunt small burrowing animals. By placing the mouth of the talisman next to his own, the hunter obtained the magical breath of the hunter god, allowing him to charm his prey. At the kill, he cut open the heart of the dead animal and bathed the fetish in the warm blood to further strengthen its power.*

MOLE—HUNTER GOD OF THE UNDERWORLD

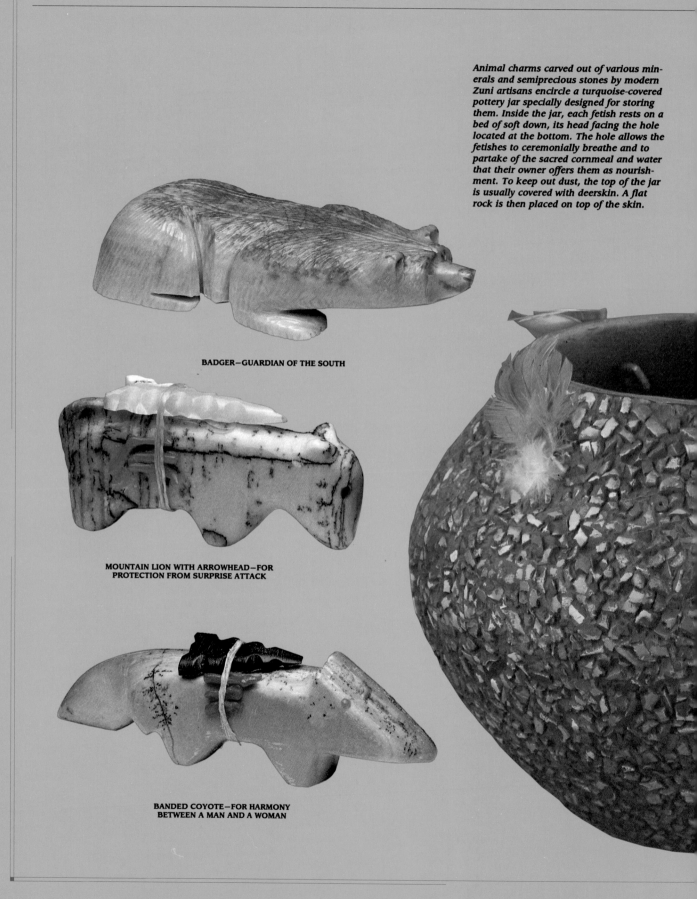

Animal charms carved out of various minerals and semiprecious stones by modern Zuni artisans encircle a turquoise-covered pottery jar specially designed for storing them. Inside the jar, each fetish rests on a bed of soft down, its head facing the hole located at the bottom. The hole allows the fetishes to ceremonially breathe and to partake of the sacred cornmeal and water that their owner offers them as nourishment. To keep out dust, the top of the jar is usually covered with deerskin. A flat rock is then placed on top of the skin.

BADGER—GUARDIAN OF THE SOUTH

MOUNTAIN LION WITH ARROWHEAD—FOR
PROTECTION FROM SURPRISE ATTACK

BANDED COYOTE—FOR HARMONY
BETWEEN A MAN AND A WOMAN

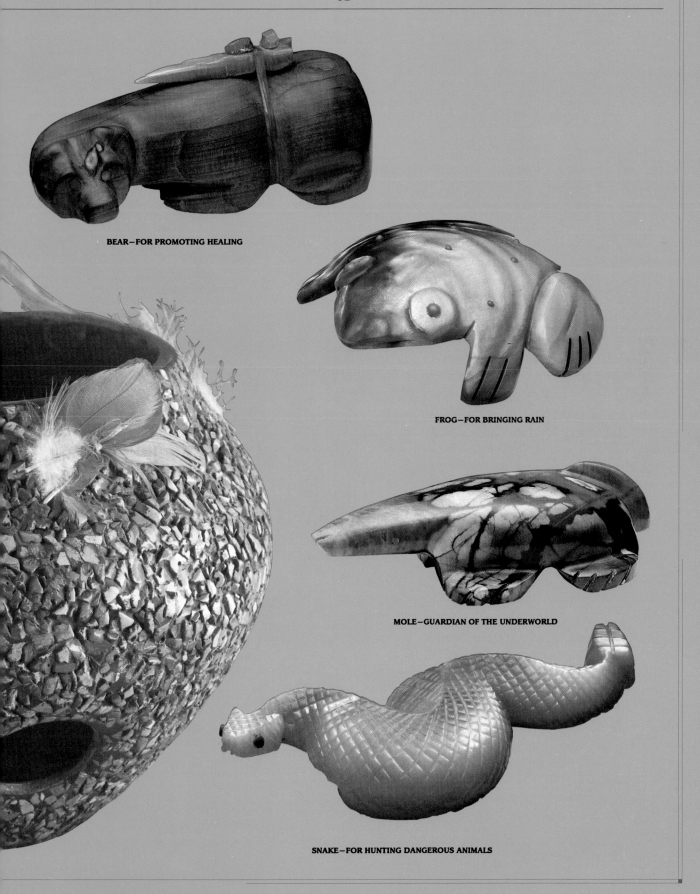

BEAR—FOR PROMOTING HEALING

FROG—FOR BRINGING RAIN

MOLE—GUARDIAN OF THE UNDERWORLD

SNAKE—FOR HUNTING DANGEROUS ANIMALS

them still reside in the single pueblo called Zuni, now a sprawl of single-story buildings rather than a multilevel complex as in earlier times. Beyond the pueblo are four small satellite settlements that offer easier access to fields and grazing lands. The reservation embraces a little more than 400,000 acres, some of it high country reaching east and north to the Zuni Mountains, some low and drier. Nine-tenths of the land is devoted to raising livestock; of the remainder, a bit is cultivated by irrigation and the rest farmed by the same techniques the Hopi use to win a living from their arid land.

In the same manner as the Hopi, Zuni society is organized into clans. The clan arrangement, according to Zuni legend, was worked out in ancient days by divine twins, progeny of the sun god. The story of that act of supernatural guidance was recorded in the late 19th century by an ethnologist named Frank Hamilton Cushing, who lived among the Zuni for several years and learned their language: "Gathering the first Priest Fathers in council, the Beloved Twins met with them to select and name groups of men and the kinds of creatures and things . . . Those who loved the sun became the Sun People, others who loved the water became the Frog, Turtle, or Toad clans . . . The Winter People according to their natures, talents, and inclinations became the Bear, the Coyote, and the Deer people . . . In this way the people were divided into clans, brothers and sisters who may not marry and who will cherish each other's offspring as their own." Although property is inherited through both the maternal and paternal lines, the matrilineal side dominates. As among the Hopi, Zuni women own the fields, the houses, and any property accumulated during a marriage, and women tend to have the final say in economic matters.

The clan system is only one element in an extremely complicated social structure. Along with 14 matrilineal clans, Zuni society includes 12

*This buffalo kachina, holding a rattle in its right hand and a lightning stick in its left, was created by Zuni artisans around 1890. Its purpose was to increase the number of furbearing animals for hunters.*

secret medicine societies that worship particular supernaturals and are believed to have powers to cure illnesses and perform deeds beyond ordinary human capability, such as dancing on hot coals without being burned, or bathing in the icy water of a river in the winter, or swallowing swords or arrows. Each of these esoteric societies has its own priesthood, meeting place, secret lore, and yearly cycle of ceremonies. One additional society has a sort of overarching status: Its members are charged with representing kachinas and other supernatural figures in masked dances; every Zuni male must be initiated into the group. Finally, hereditary, clan-linked priesthoods are responsible for summoning rain and also for providing the religious government, which complements a secular government made up of elected officials.

All of these groups are independent, but they function in concert, forming a single intertwined, overlapping system of religious belief and observance. The complexity of this system may be a consequence of the long-ago merging of six Zuni villages into one. In any case, it makes for a prodigiously rich ceremonial life, both private and public. The Kachina Society, for example, may stage productions on as many as 100 days in a single year. Its membership is spread among the Zuni's six kivas, and every kiva is expected to put on four dances during the year—in the summer, at harvesttime, shortly before the winter solstice, and during the winter. In their performances, the kachinas sing for rain, pray for the fertility of the fields or for success in the hunt, and sometimes even whip spectators in order to purify them. Masked dances range from elaborate recapitulations of the Zuni past to more impromptu affairs conducted outside the house of a person who is ill.

The most important occasion on the Zuni ritual calendar is the Shalako Ceremony, climaxing in late November or early December. During this elaborate ritual—which lasts 49 days in all its phases and requires participants to spend many months learning prayers and making other preparations—the Zuni reenact the story of their migration from a sacred lake, where they lived after their emergence from the underworld, to their present home in what they call the "middle place" in the world.

The leading figures in the performance are six supernaturals called Shalakos, who are messengers of the rain gods, and 10 wise but childlike untouchables known as Mudheads. In addition, there are several other types of supporting kachinas, all awesome in their costumes and movements. Traditionally, eight houses are constructed or extensively renovated as a way of honoring and welcoming the spirit beings: Six are for the

Shalakos, one for the Mudheads, and one for the "council of the gods."

Early in the morning of the climactic day of the ceremony, the impersonators slip away from the village, carrying their masks under blankets. That afternoon, they begin to return. First comes the fire god, impersonated by a boy of the Badger Clan whose body is painted black and dotted with the sun colors of red, yellow, blue, and white. He crosses the Zuni River on a footbridge and tours six shrines in the village, depositing prayer sticks and performing cleansing rituals. Then, heralded by the sound of a rattle, the other gods enter the village from the south, attired

*Zuni Shalakos, giant couriers of the rain gods, make their way to a dancing ground accompanied by their attendants during a ceremony that reenacts the story of the creation of the Zuni people. The painting at right shows the elaborate costumes in detail: Adorned with eagle and raven feathers, the 10-foot-tall masks are carried on poles concealed beneath the colorful draperies.*

in masks of symbolic colors, wearing turquoise jewelry, and carrying such objects as deer bones and yucca whips. Villagers sprinkle them with cornmeal as they begin their own tour of the six shrines in the pueblo. Later, as the sun sets, the Shalakos appear from around the shoulder of a hill, cross the bridge, and enter the village. They are huge and magnificent, standing about 10 feet tall and carrying their masks on a long pole. Each mask is painted turquoise, topped with a horsehair wig and eagle feathers, and fitted with two horns and a long beak that can be opened and closed by strings to make a clacking noise. The body of the costume, concealing the dancer, consists of embroidered robes wrapped around a cone-shaped hoop framework about four feet in diameter at the bottom. So heavy and unwieldy is the superstructure that each Shalako requires two impersonators to take turns in the costume, with a helper standing by to steer the rain messengers through the movements of the ceremony.

The night is filled with rituals dramatizing and explaining how the Zuni found their way to the center of the cosmos. From midnight to dawn, the Shalakos, the Mudheads, and the other kachinas dance in their respective houses as singers chant and drums throb. When the sun rises, the masked figures are sprinkled with cornmeal, and then they stop to rest. That afternoon, they depart from the village, but one last rite remains: In a field beyond the river, the great, birdlike Shalakos hold a race, moving in slow motion to a series of shrines where they deposit prayer sticks in homage to the forces that control the health, happiness, and prosperity of the Zuni. Then the Shalakos and other kachinas are gone, and the Zuni devote themselves to a week of joyful dancing and celebration that brings their ceremonial year to an end.

**T**he Western Pueblos include two other communities, Acoma and Laguna. Acoma is an ancient defensive masterpiece—a multistory complex of stone and adobe, sited on an isolated mesa 357 feet high and 70 acres in area. It is now mainly used for ceremonial purposes; most of the people of Acoma live in housing developments below the mesa. Laguna, located 15 miles to the northeast on the north bank of the San Jose River, is much larger, with a population exceeding 5,000, second only to Zuni among Pueblo communities in New Mexico. In both, the language is Keresan, but the social organization and culture of Acoma and Laguna resemble the Hopi and Zuni lifestyle in many respects, no doubt reflecting considerable contact in the past. Mat-

*With eyes closed in concentration, a clay storyteller doll tells an ancient tale to the gaggle of children draped over its body. Produced throughout the Eastern Pueblo communities, the dolls represent family continuity and the cultural tradition of passing down stories from generation to generation.*

rilineal clans and the maternal household are the chief elements of the social structure, and kachinas have the same sort of ritual prominence that is seen in the Hopi villages and at Zuni.

Farther east, along the Rio Grande and its tributaries, are five other Keresan communities, all classed with the Eastern Pueblos. Matrilineal clans exist in their societies but are markedly weaker. Property is not controlled by the clans, and a newly married man does not necessarily move to his wife's household. Nor do the clans play a governing role in the ceremonial life of the pueblo. Instead, religious activities are divided between the community's two kivas, each associated with several clans as well as with curing societies. The curing societies are especially prominent in the Eastern Keresan world, responsible not just for dealing with illnesses but also for maintaining the fertility of the earth, protecting the community from witchcraft, and overseeing ceremonies.

All of the remaining Eastern Pueblos speak one of the three versions of the Tanoan language family: Tiwa, Tewa, and Towa. Among these communities as well, matrilineal clans fill roles of reduced importance, and some of these peoples have no clans at all. To an even greater extent than among the Keresan speakers, their societies have a dual structure: Each pueblo is organized into two roughly equal divisions, variously called Winter and Summer people, or North and South people. Within a village, each group has its own kiva (or sometimes several kivas), and the divisions take turns overseeing the pueblo, exercising control in both religious and governmental spheres.

Among the Eastern Pueblos, the kachinas are of diminished importance; masked dances of these spirit beings tend to be held privately or not at all. In contrast to the Western Pueblos' intense ceremonial focus on agriculture and the fertility of the earth, the Eastern Pueblos place a strong emphasis on hunting traditions, and they hold their important festivals in the autumn and winter, when the work of farming is suspended. Big game, such as buffalo, deer, antelope, elk, and mountain sheep, always provided a larger proportion of the food supply in the east, and the availability of river water for irrigation lessened the vulnerability to agricultural setbacks. Even though communal hunts are a thing of the past, animals and humans remain linked by sacred bonds, and the hunting fes-

# THE ART OF THE PUEBLO POTTERS

Pottery making is a centuries-old tradition among the Pueblo peoples. Composed of the earth's most basic elements, pots and jars are not only essential for holding water and seeds—the sustainers of life itself—but they also are possessed of a profound spirituality. To the Pueblo Indian, clay is alive—the very stuff of which the gods created humankind. Potters pray to it and speak softly in its presence to prevent their voices from trespassing in their creations.

Twentieth-century artisans have revived this ancient craft, most pueblos having developed their own distinctive styles of pottery based on the type of local soil available and on individual technique. Some of the finest examples of their work are illustrated here.

*María Martínez (above) of San Ildefonso Pueblo molds a pot using the age-old method of building the sides with coils of clay. In 1925 she became the first Pueblo potter to sign her work, a significant step in advancing Indian pottery as an art form. She made the black-on-black storage jar at right, using a firing technique her husband Julian perfected. It substituted animal dung for wood—a technique still used by their descendants today.*

A large, round-bottomed cooking pot made in Picuris Pueblo glows with the red-gold color of the micaceous clay found in the hills near the ancient pueblo. The potters of Picuris and nearby Taos do not paint their wares but instead decorate their glittering surfaces with molded ridges of clay.

The incised design and traditional red-on-tan format of the jar at left is the hallmark of the modern pottery that is made in San Juan Pueblo. The polychrome pot with a bird and flower motif (above) was crafted at San Juan during the 1930s.

The double neck of this redware wedding jar from Santa Clara Pueblo symbolizes the union of marriage. The bride drinks from one spout, the groom from the other.

A blackware water jug made in Santa Clara Pueblo features a bear paw emblem because of that animal's uncanny ability to locate sources of water. The wide midsection of the jug makes it easier to carry when filled.

Floral and bird designs as well as "meander bands" cover this multicolored jar made in the Zia Pueblo. Zia potters use volcanic lava as a tempering agent, causing their works to appear peppered with black flecks.

tivals rival the great western kachina dances in their drama and beauty.

A winter dance staged at the Keresan pueblo of San Felipe unfolds much like a play. The opening scene occurs at dawn, when a young female dancer—representing a spirit who attracts the game, and attended by hunters—ventures into the hills surrounding the village. There, she discovers buffalo, deer, and other animals, enacted by dancers in elaborate horned costumes. The hunters and their spirit leader pursue the prey, sprinting through the sandy hills, and at the end of the successful chase, the woman leads the game into the village. All the players then enter a kiva for secret rites, later emerging to dance in the plaza, which has been planted with small pine trees to signify a forest. Four dances are held in the morning and four in the afternoon—stately, rhythmic pantomimes in which the animals advance toward the maiden dancer, then attempt to flee, only to be lured back again by her power. At the conclusion of the dance, the woman disappears. The animals try to hide behind the pine trees, but the hunters close in, shoot a deer, pick up the fallen animal, and carry it off to a kiva: Once again, nature has provided the people of San Felipe with what they need to live.

The pueblo located closest to the nomadic, buffalo-hunting tribes of the Great Plains was Taos, and centuries of contact can be read in the way the Taos men braid their hair, in their manner of dress, and in the pueblo's styles of music and dance. The vast grasslands were not the only hunting ground utilized by the Taos Indians, however. The pueblo lies at the foot of the Sangre de Cristo mountain range, and its hunters regularly traveled into the uplands for elk, deer, bear, turkey, and other game. Because of the high altitude—more than 7,000 feet—and a short growing season, agriculture has always played a smaller part in the economy of Taos than elsewhere, and there are other distinctions as well: Clans are absent, and the organization of society into two divisions is less clearly drawn than among most peoples of the Rio Grande region. Yet Taos retains the essence of Pueblo culture in other ways—in its multistory architecture, in its people's powerful sense of obligation to the community, and in the depth of its religious life.

Within the village, ritual knowledge and observance are centered on six kivas, each with its own society. But some of the most important rituals take place outside the pueblo. Each year, individuals are expected to visit many sacred sites—springs, mountain peaks, upland lakes, and other places that figure in the mythical past of the Taos people.

The most sacred of these places—their ultimate shrine—is Blue Lake,

*In the photograph below, taken about 1900, Koshare clowns shinny up a pole in an event capping the celebration of Saint Geronimo's feast day in Taos, held every September 30. The photograph at right shows a clown claiming the sacred offerings hanging from the top of the 50-foot pole.*

the source of the pueblo's water supply. For many centuries, people of Taos annually traveled 20 miles into the mountains to make offerings of feathers, cornmeal, or turquoise, to bathe in the purifying water, and to pray for a fruitful earth, an abundance of game, and the vigor of their society. Then, in 1906, the United States government took Blue Lake and the surrounding woods and meadows away, subsequently incorporating them into Carson National Forest. The Taos Indians did not protest at first, believing that the land would be protected by the government. But the white men built roads into the area, and hunters and campers began to trample over the terrain and remove or destroy the prayer sticks left by the Indians on their annual pilgrimages. Around Blue Lake, loggers cut down trees that the Indians regarded as "living saints." The mountain meadows, a source of ritually crucial plants, were rented to cattle ranchers.

When the degree of desecration to their sacred land became clear, the Indians embarked on a campaign to regain their holiest shrine. The government's first reply, in 1926, was an offer of money to settle their claim with the sum of $297,684.67. The Indians turned it down. In 1933 Congress granted the Indians a 50-year special-use permit, but the U.S. Forest Service continued to promote recreational activities in the area, stocking the lake with trout (which fishermen sometimes slaughtered wholesale with dynamite) and constructing a camping area at the water's edge. Some 30 years later, in the 1960s, public opinion finally began to turn in favor of the Indians. A number of political leaders endorsed their cause. Newspapers across the country weighed in with supportive editorials. And the National Council of Churches declared: "What the Indians of Taos Pueblo are asking is that equal consideration, no more no less, be extended to the shrine where they have performed their religious obligations for at least as long as the famed cathedrals of Europe have been in use."

On December 2, 1970, the U.S. Senate voted overwhelmingly to return Blue Lake and 48,000 surround-

ing acres to the Indians. At the time the bill was signed into law, the mission bell was rung at Taos to announce the long-awaited news, and afterward a dance was held, celebrating the victory with the ancient sounds of drums, rattles, and chanting.

The greeting of such news by both a mission bell and drums is symptomatic of the layered makeup of Pueblo culture today. Although the Indians of Taos are deeply attached to their old religion and guard it by a policy of near-absolute secrecy, they, like most other Pueblos, consider themselves Catholics. In the sphere of government, change has been even more pronounced. Once, the government was purely theocratic; now it is largely secular and elected: The pueblo's 22 civil officers include a governor, lieutenant governor, and sheriff. And physically, the pueblo presents a double face to the world. The old village, multistoried and surrounded by a defensive wall that was built to fend off Comanche raiders in the 18th century, has been carefully preserved, yet many of the Taos Indians have moved outside the wall and live in separate homes, complete with fenced yards, flower beds, furniture, and modern appliances.

All across the Pueblo world, cultural crosscurrents, compromises, and even contradictions are apparent. The Indians use tractors and other farming machinery to work fields they once cultivated by hand. Many people hold wage-earning jobs, whether on reservation lands or in non-Indian communities. Tourism is an important ingredient of the Pueblo economy, and arts and crafts—jewelry making, pottery, weaving, basket making, the carving of kachina dolls—are major sources of income. The young attend school and speak English; in some of the less conservative pueblos, many of the children do not understand their ancestral language at all. Even among such conservative matrilineal communities as the Hopi villages, a large number of young couples now move into their own homes and raise their families separate from the maternal clan. And increasingly, the Hopi schedule their ceremonies to accommodate the weekly work pattern of wage earners.

With reason, the elders worry that some of the young people are drifting away from their Indian heritage, and disputes between the generations are a cause of social strain in certain communities. But as long as the old ceremonies are held in the plaza and kivas, the currents of modernity will stir only the surface of the Pueblo world. No matter how strong, those currents cannot touch the depths—the sanctuary of the Pueblo self. That portion of their world is constructed around ideas of perpetuation and permanence. It is timeless. ✣

# SEASONS OF THE KACHINAS

To obtain the precious water they need to survive on their parched land, the Hopi rely on the help of supernatural beings who dwell in a realm of mist and magic that is as gentle and as moist as the mesas are harsh and dry. These are the kachinas, the spirit essences of everything on earth. For half of the year, there is only ephemeral evidence of their existence—in the steam rising from a hot meal or the morning mist hovering over a spring. But in the six months between the winter and summer solstices, the kachinas leave their homes in the cloud-topped San Francisco Peaks and enter the Hopi villages in material form in order to take part in ceremonies held annually to get the growing season off to a successful start.

During this earthly sojourn, they are personified by costumed men in masks believed to invest the wearers with specific kachina spirits. Carved dolls (pictured at left and on the following pages) duplicate the dancers. They are often used to teach children to distinguish among the hundreds of kachina spirits. Some, such as those representing the spirits of departed ancestors, are purely local. A few represent gods, although kachinas themselves are not worshiped as deities. They are regarded instead as valued friends whose connection to the natural forces controlling rain and fertility makes them key allies in the endless struggle to produce food.

*The Masau kachina reigns over the earth and the underworld. All those who use the land are required to pay respect to this spirit, who also controls the emergence of kachinas into the mortal world.*

*The chosen Soyal chief, who presides over the solstice observances, casts sacred cornmeal over three kachinas. The two holding corn bundles are*

## A PRAYER FOR THE NEW YEAR

In late December, a solitary masked figure dressed in tattered buckskin totters into the Hopi village, singing feebly. He staggers as if he has just awakened from a long sleep. This is Soyal kachina, first of the masked spirits to emerge from the kachinas' mountain home. He is the herald of Soyal, the nine-day winter solstice ceremony.

Soyal marks the beginning of the new year, when the Hopi cast off the ills of the old season and ask for good fortune in the new. Its central event is the ceremonial opening of the kivas, a task initiated by the Soyal kachina and completed by other kachinas who appear on the ceremony's final day. From then on, the kachinas are nearby and may visit the village at any time.

*Mastop kachina, representing fertility, bounds into the village on the next to last day of Soyal, exuberantly simulating intercourse with women he grabs from among the onlookers.*

*mana kachinas, who are impersonating women.*

# CELEBRATING THE SEEDS

The February new moon marks the beginning of Powamu, or the Bean Dance, a celebration of germination and growth. Powamu is a plea to the kachinas to act on behalf of the seeds that will be planted. It is also the time when children are initiated into the kachina cult. In a ceremony presided over by Crow Mother kachina and her sons the whipper twins, the six- to 10-year-olds learn for the first time that the masked dancers are men, not spirits.

On the last day of Powamu, Crow Mother walks through the village carrying a basket of bean shoots, portents of abundance, that have been forced to sprout in the hothouselike kivas.

*The horned Hu' kachina with bared teeth and bulging eyes is one of the whipper twins who ritually lash children with yucca fronds as part of their Powamu initiation ceremony.*

*Crow Mother kachina, "the one with crow tied on," wears crow wings on her mask. She holds the basket of bean sprouts symbolizing the miracle of germination in the midst of winter.*

*Menacing Soyoko kachinas, who during Pow-*

*mu terrorize disobedient children by threatening to eat them, surround a kiva hatch to demand meat from the kiva chief.*

The runner kachina known as Dung Carrier, is said to stuff dry dung into the mouths of those he defeats in footraces.

Wearing a peaked hat suggestive of the thunderheads he is believed to control, the Heart of Sky God appears carrying crossed sticks that represent lightning.

Bearded kachinas, whose beards represent falling rain, assemble for a line dance in which they all wear the same costume. They are flanked by mana kachinas acting as wives and sisters.

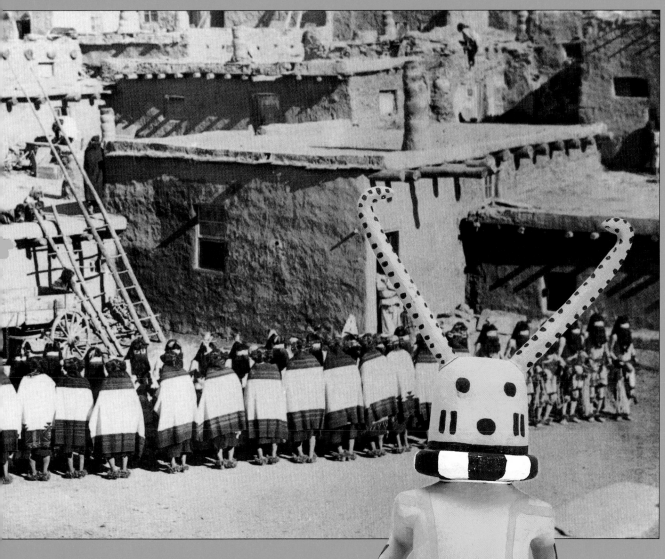

## SPRINGTIME RITES BEFORE PLANTING

Every spring, the central plaza of each Hopi village is the site of daylong dances that precede planting. The 40 to 60 kachinas who typically take part are thought to bring the moisture of the spirit world with them. They appear 12 to 14 times during the day, chanting assurances such as the one expressed in this blessing: "Listen, listen my friends. Don't lose faith in me. Pray to me. I, in reply with water downpouring, will keep you alive."

During breaks between dances, the crowd feasts, plays games, and laughs at the antics of capering clowns. Runner kachinas challenge male spectators to footraces—with the losers often suffering mortifying consequences.

*The horned runner, Scorpion kachina, is also called Throwing Stick Man, a name believed to derive from the arachnid's manner of flipping its tail in order to sting.*

At about noon on the day of a plaza dance, the clown kachinas appear in the village to entertain the assembled crowd. Tripping and stumbling over one another, they gather in the plaza, where they irreverently pelt the dancers with cornmeal and shout out rude questions. They call to each other in raucous tones and squabble noisily over morsels of food, mocking the rules of propriety that govern everyday life in the normally restrained and moderate Hopi society.

During breaks in the ceremony, the clown kachinas mimic the dancers, employing obscene and lewd gestures, and they elicit appreciative laughs from the onlookers with burlesque performances designed to ridicule everyone from schoolteachers to government officials to the camera-laden tourists who come to observe their ritual.

Clown kachinas enter the plaza by clambering unsteadily over the rooftops, amusing spectators with their stumbling descent (left). The clown Mudhead (below, left), a popular feature of nearly every kachina dance, plays games with the town's children during breaks in the ceremonies.

Koshare, or Hano clowns, are distinguished by their bold stripes (right), and act out embarrassing extremes of behavior. Those below make fools of themselves in a slapstick tug of war.

Snow Kachina Girl, also called White Kachina Girl, often appears at Niman dances. She personifies a prayer that the coming cold weather will bring snowfalls to replenish the earth with moisture.

Hemis kachina, thought to bring high-growing corn, wears a headdress of wooden panels painted with fertility symbols and decked with eagle feathers and imitation corn tassels. He shakes a gourd rattle to evoke the sound of rain.

# DANCING DOWN THE RAIN

By July the first ears of corn are ripening in the fields, and the rain-filled thunderheads have gathered in the summer skies. These are the unmistakable signs that the kachinas have completed their work, and it is time for them to return to their mountain home.

Their departure is marked by the solemn Niman Ceremony, held at the summer solstice. After eight days of secret rites in the kivas, the kachinas appear in the plaza for one last public dance and a final prayerful appeal for rain in the coming months. Then at sundown, the village chiefs deliver their farewells to the departing spirits, who slowly file out of town on a path of cornmeal that has been laid out for them pointing west toward the San Francisco Peaks. No one moves until the last kachina is out of sight.

*A line of stately Hemis kachinas dances at Niman, their exalted status reinforced by the towering headdresses that seem to lift them up toward the rain-giving sky.*

# FACES OF THE DESERT

Photographed around 1900, the Native Americans seen on the following pages represent cultures as diverse as the mesas, mountains, and canyons that they occupied. Warring and trading with each other over a period of hundreds of years, these tribes populated the great Southwest, an area that stretches from the Rio Grande to the Mojave Desert, and from the Sierra Madre to the southern Rocky Mountains.

Descendants of an ancient people that occupied the region for millennia, the Pueblo Indians developed a highly communal lifestyle in villages that dotted the landscape from the Painted Desert to the Rio Grande. By the 15th century, newcomers to the region, having migrated southward for generations, had virtually surrounded the Pueblos. Some of these nomadic groups, who came to be known as the Apaches and Navajos, raided their sedentary neighbors continually, but began gradually to adopt many of their ways. To the south and west of the Pueblos were other longtime residents of the region, hardy peoples who had settled along the deltas and banks of the lower Colorado and Gila and Salt rivers, and some who eked out a living in surrounding upland areas. In distinctive ways, these peoples have been influenced by contact with one another and with the European newcomers. All have adapted remarkably well to the unrelenting demands of the Southwest—its searing heat, protracted droughts, torrential downpours, and bitter cold. All are the faces of the desert.

MOHAVE CHIEF

HOPI MAIDEN ▶

APACHE GIRL

HOSHKAY YAZHIE, NAVAJO MEDICINE MAN  ▶

LA LE LA, ZUNI GOVERNOR

◄ OHWO-WO-SONGWI, SAN ILDEFONSO DANCER

SELFON, ACOMA MAN

◄ MARICOPA WOMAN

MARICOPA WARRIOR

LIETA, PIMA WOMAN  ▶

2

# KINDRED TRIBES IN A DAUNTING LAND

*The legacy of a centuries-old craft, a Pima basketwork tray is made from dried willow branches coiled around cattails. The labyrinth design, common to both the Pima and Papago, illustrates the story of the deity Elder Brother, whose house, represented by the central circle, can be reached only by following the correct path.*

The gold seekers following the southern route to California were in a torment of apprehension on this July day in 1849. They had last filled their casks and watered their animals many miles back, not far from Tucson, where the Santa Cruz River sank ominously into the sands. Ahead lay a seemingly endless desert, bleak, blazing, and all but devoid of forage. The wagon tracks stretched away to an empty horizon. Men began to abandon their staggering livestock and draft animals.

This desolate expanse below the upper Gila River was Indian country, and the forty-niners knew it. Everyone kept a worried eye out for an ambush. The Apache were greatly feared. Two other tribes in the area, the Pima and the Maricopa, were said to be friendly. Yet who could be sure?

"Indians!" someone shouted—and there they were, blocking the trail ahead. But then dread dissolved into sighs of relief as the Indians could be heard shouting, "Amigos! Amigos!" They were Pima tribesmen, and true to their reputation, several came forward holding out gourds filled with water for the parched travelers. Others offered roasted pumpkins and green corn and—incredibly—large, sweet, juicy watermelons. The obliging Pima even retrieved, fed, and watered the abandoned livestock. With beckoning gestures, they encouraged the forty-niners to follow the wagon ruts; the Gila River lay a short distance ahead. Later, at the river, the Pima thronged to the miners' camps, trading melons and baskets of beans and maize for beads, blankets, and clothing. Then the Indians sped the grateful but somewhat bewildered prospectors on their way.

The forty-niners were not alone in their puzzlement over the Indians in this part of the Southwest. As late as the mid-19th century, 300 years after the first contacts with Europeans, few people in the United States knew much about the Pima and kindred communities inhabiting what is now Arizona and the northern Mexican states of Sonora, Sinaloa, Chihuahua, and Durango. At home in settings that outsiders found brutally inhospitable, they were not easily subjugated. To be sure, they had faced

many incursions over the centuries—first by the Spaniards, then by the Mexicans, and now by Anglo-Americans. Yet their tenacity and, in some cases, their ferocity had made it difficult for intruders to dominate them.

These resilient desert peoples consisted of two basic groups, separated by latitude and language. The Pima and tribes to their south—including the Yaqui and Mayo who lived along rivers flowing into the Gulf of California, and the Tepehuan and Tarahumara who occupied the steep canyons and rugged uplands of the Sierra Madre—spoke languages of the Uto-Aztecan family, which included the official language of the former Aztec Empire. To the north and west of the Pima lived tribes belonging to the Yuman language family, including valley dwellers such as the Maricopa, Quechan, and Mohave who flanked the Gila and Colorado rivers, and inhabitants of upland Arizona such as the Yavapai and the related Hualapai and Havasupai. Together, these tribes covered a vast area embracing a daunting diversity of terrain, from sand-swept depressions that blazed like furnaces from May through October to precipitous heights where even midsummer nights could be chilling. Yet the far-flung peoples responded to the challenges of their surroundings in similar ways, deftly coaxing a living from often-desolate terrain, enlivening the harsh regimens with spirited festivities, and sharing their hard-earned bounty with friends as readily as they defended their domain against enemies.

No one knows for certain where the Pima came from. They may well have descended from the ancient Hohokam (Pima for "those who are gone"), an accomplished people who established their first settlements in the region more than 2,000 years ago. Over the centuries, the Hohokam constructed a remarkable network of irrigation canals extending for more than 500 miles across the Gila and Salt river basins. Near their well-watered fields, they built solid earthen dwellings to supplement their earlier pole-and-thatch huts, laid out courts and plazas for ball games and ceremonies, and erected massive platform mounds crowned by temples and storehouses. After thriving in the desert for more than a millennium, the Hohokam mysteriously declined around AD 1400. Sapped by drought,

*A Pima record rod five and a half feet long bears carved symbols that help a chronicler remember dates and events in the village's history. The span between each notch represents a year as reckoned from the July saguaro cactus harvest; the chronicler, who "reads" the rod by feel as well as by sight, can retell the detailed story of each year.*

famine, or other stresses, their complex society collapsed. Some of the survivors may have migrated to distant areas while others remained behind to become the modern Pima.

Whatever their ancestry, people speaking the Piman language inherited a vast territory of approximately 24,000 square miles, extending from the head of the Gulf of California in the west to the Arizona-New Mexico border in the east, and from the Gila-Salt river basin in the north to Yaqui territory in the south. All Pima Indians referred to themselves simply as *O'odham,* or "the People." But within this broad category, three separate groups emerged, each of them practicing a different survival strategy within a distinct ecological zone.

At the far western edge of Pima country, along the Gulf of California, lies one of the lowest, hottest, and driest deserts in North America, an unforgiving place where summer temperatures soar to 120 degrees Fahrenheit and rainfall averages less than five inches a year. Some years no rain falls at all. It is a land of small-leaved, drought-resistant plants, some cactus, and few animals. When Spaniards first crossed this wasteland in the 17th century, they encountered the *Hiatatk O'odham,* or "Sand People," who eked out a living there in small seminomadic bands. Some of them farmed plots along the Colorado and other waterways feeding into the gulf, but they subsisted mainly by hunting for sparse game and scrounging for edibles along the banks of foothill arroyos. In the 1690s, a Spanish traveler characterized them as "poor and hungry" and contended that they were "little given to work," although he conceded that they made the most of their limited resources: "They live on the roots and wild fruits which the region produces at various times of the year. They also eat shellfish, worms, lizards, iguanas, and other animals considered repugnant by us. At certain seasons of the year, they live on fish from the Gulf of California." Over the years, the ranks of these hard-pressed Sand People diminished to a precious few.

Farther east in a hillier region of Sonora, average rainfall increases to as much as 10 inches annually, and intermittent rivers and streams meander through a landscape of paloverde and mesquite, with abundant prickly pear, cholla, and towering saguaro cactus. Springs are numerous, providing water for the deer, mountain sheep, peccaries, doves, rabbits, and other small game that abound in the area. Here, early Spanish explorers encountered a people called the *Tohono O'odham,* or "Desert People," who migrated back and forth from summer encampments near flood-watered fields to winter homes near mountain springs. The Spaniards estimated that there were 12,000 of these Indians and referred to them as *papabotas,* or "bean eaters," a term that was eventually abridged to Papago, the name by which they are generally known today. Their society was a triumph of adaptation.

During the months of July and August, when thunderheads billowed on the horizon, the Papago toiled in valley fields near arroyos to prepare the land for growing crops. At the mouth of each wash, they built brush dams to spread the runoff from periodic cloudbursts to the waiting fields. When the soil had been well watered, the men planted corn, beans, and squash. Before and during planting, parties of women guarded by armed men foraged extensively for the stems, leaves, flowers, roots, bulbs, nuts, or fruits of the region's many edible plants.

Of all the desert's bounty, the Papago prized the saguaro cactus most highly. The ripening of the saguaro fruit in late June or early July marked the New Year, in observance of which the people staged a sacred ceremony designed to "bring down the clouds." Women armed with picks made from long saguaro ribs plucked the fruit from the high limbs of the cactus and collected it in baskets. Some of the spiny, plumlike fruit was eaten raw, and some of it was dried. The women also strained the crimson pulp into ceramic pots and boiled it to produce a sweet syrup. After the harvest, the community's ritual leaders fermented the syrup into a wine called *nawait.* Three or four days of imbibing followed, when the sacred obligation of every man was to get drunk and vomit and urinate freely so as to return the precious liquid to the dry earth—an outpouring designed to ensure the summer rains.

Following the New Year's festivities and the planting of crops, the Papago continued to camp in brush houses near the fields as long as their supply of captured water lasted. If they were lucky, the ponds held out until the crops ripened during the dry days of autumn. Traditionally, the harvest supplied about one-third of their food needs. Whatever corn, beans, and squash they did not consume on the spot would be dried and stored in grass baskets, which were then carried away when the people decamped to sites near water sources in the foothills. There they re-

*Silhouetted against the sky, a Papago couple harvests the sweet red fruit of a giant saguaro, knocking down the pods with a pole made from dried cactus ribs (above). The flesh is scooped out, boiled, and poured through a strainer to remove the seeds (inset, right). The empty husks are placed facedown on the ground to entice summer rains.*

*The strained juice from the saguaro fruit is mixed with yeast and kept warm over a slow fire for three to four days in a ceremonial rain house (above, background), where villagers gather to sing and dance while the liquid ferments. The structure in front of the rain house is a ramada, providing shade.*

mained through winter and the arid days of spring, supplementing foodstuffs drawn from their larder by hunting and gathering until the time came to return to their fields and renew the annual cycle.

Hard times might befall a Papago village while another nearby settlement prospered. The tender shoots in one field might be swamped by runoff from a torrential downpour, for example, while a distant plot received just the right amount of moisture. But the people had an admirable way of offering the unfortunate a chance to recoup. A village in want could place a claim on the food supplies of its luckier neighbors, the issue to be decided by men on horseback, champion runners, or other athletes. The challenging village would bet its blankets and livestock on the outcome, in the hope of winning an equal value in food. The challengers had to be sure of their champions; if they lost, the village would be much worse off than before. But a second custom usually kept people from going hungry: The destitute village could perform a Begging Dance lasting several nights—and be rewarded with generous gifts of food from the prosperous winners. Through such rituals, the people acknowledged that nature could be fickle with its bounty and that those who had plenty one year might need help from their neighbors the next.

What the Papago were unable to obtain through foraging, farming, hunting—and gambling on their athletic competitions—they acquired through trade or ceremonial gift exchange. Precious salt, which they gathered during annual pilgrimages to salt pans along the Gulf of California, was a much-traded item, as were pots, buckskins, dried meat, and dried saguaro fruit or syrup. When trade items were scarce, the Papago performed rain and fertility ceremonies in neighboring villages in exchange for a portion of the harvest. Within villages, reciprocal gift giving was a time-honored way of distributing resources. When a man returned from a hunting expedition with a deer, for example, his neighbor might present him with a small quantity of beans, which prompted a gift of venison in return. The man who had killed the deer might come out on the short end of the bargain, but he knew that he would benefit from a similar exchange if his neighbor made a catch in the future.

From time to time, explorers, prospectors, and missionaries passed through Papago territory. One renowned and indefatigable Jesuit proselytizer, Father Eusebio Kino, traversed the area in the late 17th century and wrote admiringly of the Indians. But Father Kino and his successors preferred to work in fertile river valleys, where irrigation could be practiced and sizable populations gathered in one spot. A number of Papago were drawn into such riverine missions elsewhere, and they learned new farming techniques and livestock herding. Subsequently, some of them established cattle ranches in the vicinity.

The land that attracted the early missionaries was the domain of the *Akimel O'odham,* or "River People," who occupied permanent settlements in the rich alluvial plains of the Gila and its more dependable tributaries. Those arteries retained water for much of their length throughout the year and supported a cornucopia of plant and animal life. The grassy highlands stretching between the rivers received as much as 15 inches of rain annually. These people built their villages on natural terraces above the rivers; in addition, they occupied summer camps of thatched huts alongside their fields in order to protect the crops from pests and thieves, and ventured abroad for weeks at a time during other seasons to hunt and gather. They shared many of the customs of the Papago, including the New Year saguaro festival.

It was into this land of relative plenty that Father Kino rode his horse in 1687. Avid horticulturalists, the River People derived as much as 60 percent of their diet from crops cultivated along the rich bottom lands. Typically, the rivers flooded several times a year—once in early spring when snow melted in the mountains and again after heavy downpours in the summer. The River People planted corn, beans, pumpkins, and other crops in March, when the fields were moist from the spring floods. Most of those crops were harvested by June. Then in July, it was time to lay down a second planting for a fall harvest.

The River People maintained effective local irrigation systems, using techniques that they may have inherited from the ancient Hohokam. Along the Gila, they constructed dams of stones, poles, and branches for diverting floodwaters into a maze of ditches feeding the fields. About once every five years in most places, drought or catastrophic flooding made it impossible to harvest a crop. But the Pima were expert survivalists. When their stores ran low, they simply intensified the hunting and gathering activities that normally supplied about 40 percent of their food. The thickets of mesquite trees that crowded the river valleys yielded nutritious pods in abundance. These they supplemented with cactus fruit and whatever game could be had. Like the Papago, they had begging dances and other ceremonies for distributing bounty.

Father Kino's great gift to the River People was winter wheat. Planted in late fall and harvested in the spring, it provided the Indians with a bonanza in an otherwise-lean season and served as insurance against the failure of other crops. Such life-sustaining beneficence may have helped the missionaries attract Indians to the church. At first, Father Kino rode from village to village with a few other priests, interpreters, and military escorts, setting up altars and calling for converts. Within two years, he had baptized 800 Pimas and founded a mission at Dolores on the San Miguel River. By 1710, a year before his death, there were three missions in the area and more than a dozen stations visited by priests. A late entry in his journal reflects the material success of these ventures: "There are already very rich and abundant fields, plantings, and crops of wheat, maize, and frijoles. There are good gardens, and in them vineyards for wine for Masses, with canebrakes of sweet cane for syrup. There are many Castilian fruit trees, such as fig trees, quinces, oranges, and plentiful ranches stocked with cattle, sheep, and goats, and abundant pastures all the year to raise very fat sheep."

Like the Pueblo Indians to the northeast, the River People found that the benefits of colonization were accompanied by grievous ills—including lethal epidemics of smallpox, measles, and scarlet fever. Yet they managed to persevere as a distinct culture. The missionaries, for all their influence, could not induce the people to forsake their local shamans. Pima shamans were specialists. Some performed ceremonies to influence the weather, others brought warriors success in battle, and a third group diagnosed diseases caused by the angry spirits of animals and other natural forces. The Spanish priests could absolve people who were thought to have sinned against man or God, but only shamans could help those who had offended the spirit of a bear by stepping in its tracks or incurred the wrath of a snake by thoughtlessly treading on its burrow.

On a few occasions, Pima villagers who felt that their own rights or traditions had been trampled upon rose up against the demanding missionaries, executing priests and sacking churches before meeting with harsh reprisals from armed Spaniards. But the Indians and white men had a common enemy to consider—the Apache, who cast acquisitive eyes on the region's flourishing fields and herds. Although the Pima lacked any central authority—each village saw to its own affairs—they united militarily against the threat. Settlements posted sentinels along likely Apache approach routes and developed daily military drills for all adult males. By 1800 the region was defended by a combined army of 1,000 warriors. Forty years later, the Pima were the only effective restraint against Apache raiding in southern Arizona and northwestern Mexico.

The Pima along the Gila River extended their protection to the thousands of white fur trappers and gold diggers who passed through their country. Efforts to feed and provision the westering Americans became a thriving enterprise. Records for the year 1862 show that the Indians furnished the United States government with more than one million pounds of wheat, as well as chickens, corn, and pumpkins—enough to provision 1,000 soldiers for many months.

The contributions of the Pima won them little gratitude from federal authorities. By this time, Washington regarded all territory of the various Piman speakers within U.S. borders as federal property. In 1854 the United States and Mexico, without consulting or even informing the Pima, had made final the Gadsden Purchase, by which the United States acquired nearly 30,000 square miles of land for $10 million, fixing the border where it is today. During the next several years, encroaching Mexican ranchers killed many of the Indians on the Mexican side of the new border and drove others northward into southern Arizona, where they found refuge with their kinsmen. The survivors who remained behind were largely assimilated into Mexican society. The Pima on the United States side were inclined to welcome federal control of their territories, in part because of the support it afforded against the Apache but also because of new economic opportunities that grew out of white settlement. But they had no idea of the price they would have to pay.

*In this 20th-century painting by a Papago artist, a shaman performs a "dóajida," during which he will suck sources of illness, known as "strengths," from the patient's body. The coffee can in front of the woman (right) will serve as a receptacle for the discarded strengths, which are said to take a liquid form.*

# THE PIMA WAY OF HEALING

The Pima of southern Arizona believe that an inharmonious relationship with the natural world can cause various "staying sicknesses," so named because they have existed from the beginning of time. According to tradition, Pima Indians run the risk of contracting these illnesses whenever they do something to insult one of the earth's many hazardous forces, which include bears, butterflies, even the wind. If, for example, a Pima were to crush a butterfly, it is believed that the creature's negative power would enter the offender's body, eventually triggering a disease. Each of the staying sicknesses exhibits distinctive symptoms—lice or nosebleeds for eagle sickness, stomach troubles for gopher sickness, or open sores for lightning sickness.

Once it has been determined that the ailment is the result of disharmony, treatment begins with a ceremony in which a shaman identifies and removes the sources of the illness. Then a healer—a member of the community who is not a shaman—takes over to rub the patient's body with fetishes and sing verses that appeal to the dignity of the offended forces. In certain cases, additional measures, such as sand paintings or dances, are required in order to effect a cure.

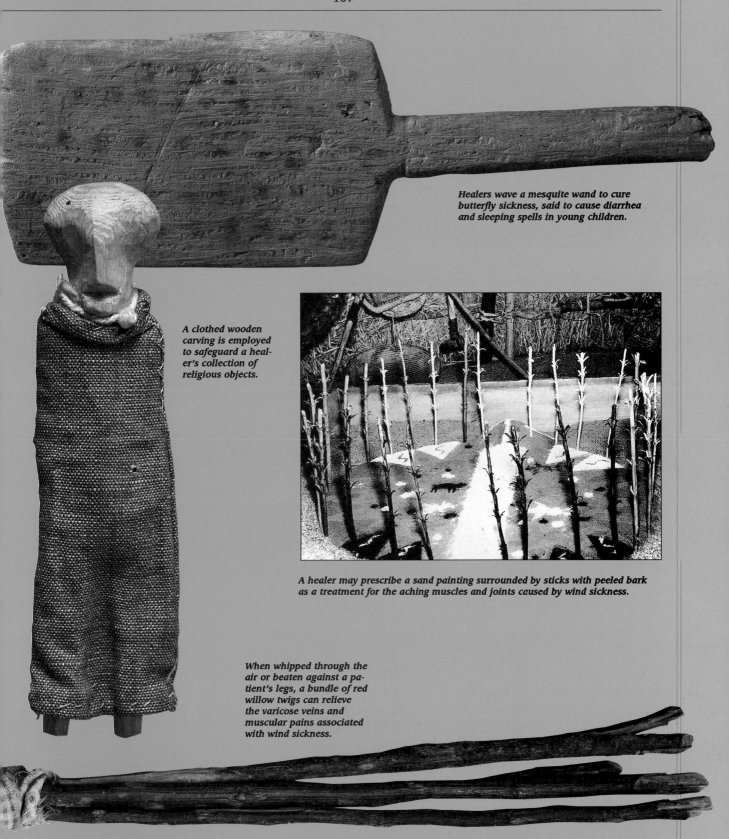

Healers wave a mesquite wand to cure butterfly sickness, said to cause diarrhea and sleeping spells in young children.

A clothed wooden carving is employed to safeguard a healer's collection of religious objects.

A healer may prescribe a sand painting surrounded by sticks with peeled bark as a treatment for the aching muscles and joints caused by wind sickness.

When whipped through the air or beaten against a patient's legs, a bundle of red willow twigs can relieve the varicose veins and muscular pains associated with wind sickness.

Between 1874 and 1917, the United States government established six Pima reservations. The Indians living along the Gila River fared the worst. American farmers upstream of the Gila River Reservation dug numerous irrigation canals along the river and began diverting its flow. Before long, Pima crops withered, and the Indians had to abandon their farms. By the 1890s, the proud O'odham agriculturalists found themselves laboring for white men in low-wage jobs. In the 1920s, the federal government responded by constructing the Coolidge Dam to catch the diminished flow of water down the Gila and divert part of it to the reservation. Some farming is still done there today, but the country is not nearly as lush as it once was.

In his memoirs, George Webb, a modern-day Pima, recalled the life enjoyed by his people before and after the white men drained the Gila: "In the old days, some Pima boy would open the head gate, and the water would flow out along the ditches. All the Pimas were in the fields with their shovels. They would fan out and lead the water to the alfalfa, along the corn rows, and over to the melons. The red-winged blackbirds would sing in the trees and fly down to look for bugs. The green of those Pima fields spread along the river for many miles in the old days. Now the river is an empty bed full of sand. Now you can stand in that same place and see the wind tearing pieces of bark off the cottonwood trees along the dry ditches. The dead trees stand there like white bones. The red-winged blackbirds have gone somewhere else."

Similar challenges awaited the descendants of the 30,000 or more Indians encountered by early Spanish explorers in the Yaqui River valley, a verdant belt descending from the foothills of the Sierra Madre to the Gulf of California. Although these Yaqui tribesmen, like the Pima to their north, were skilled flood plain farmers, they had a special genius for warfare, and their tenacity in combat earned them the grudging respect of the colonists. The Spaniards discovered early on just how fierce these people could be. In 1533 the conquistador Diego de Guzmán and a party of slave hunters were heading north when they came upon a large band of Indian warriors near the banks of the Yaqui River. The Indians drew a line in the sand, indicating that the strangers were not to cross. The Spaniards ignored the warning. In the battle that followed, Guzmán was hurled back in astonished defeat, suffering many wounded men and horses. Upon their return south, one of

A Papago woman labors under her "kihau," or burden basket, that is held in place with a forehead strap. The pack consists of a basketwork body stretched across a frame of four dried cactus ribs (inset). Legend tells that the baskets walked by themselves until Coyote, the mythical trickster, laughed at the ridiculous sight and made them a woman's burden.

the Spaniards reported that they had encountered the greatest fighters in all of New Spain.

It was a sentiment heartily echoed some
years later, around
1610, when an-
other Spanish
captain attempted to venture north beyond the
river. Three times, Diego Martínez de Hurdaide
attacked with a force of 50 or so heavily armed
Spaniards backed by a few thousand Indian
auxiliaries. Three times the Yaqui routed him.
During the third battle, 7,000 Yaquis engaged
Hurdaide's army. The Spaniards' Indian allies fled,
leaving behind a carpet of dead and wounded. Thanks
to their body armor and helmets, the Spaniards suffered
no fatalities. But every man among them was wounded. Hurdaide could count himself fortunate to escape death or capture. A
zealot who had subdued 20,000 other Indians in the decade past, Hurdaide was so shaken by the debacle that he made no further attempt to
advance Spanish rule by military means.

*This Pima war
headdress is made
of feathers from
birds of prey. Eagle
feathers were used
to symbolize swift-
ness, owl feathers
for keenness of vi-
sion by night, and
hawk feathers for
vigilance by day.*

The Yaqui were magnanimous in victory. They offered the Spaniards
peace, and when Hurdaide accepted, they returned all arms, horses, and
captives taken during the recent battles. Moreover, the Yaqui announced
that they would show their good faith by ceasing to make war on neighboring tribes. In 1616 they went a step further, inviting the Spaniards to
establish a Jesuit mission among them. The Yaqui were astute, and the
invitation may have stemmed from their observations of the Jesuits' work
among the river-dwelling Mayo to their south, a tribe similar in language
and culture. Unlike the Yaqui, the Mayo had decided at the start that accommodation was the better part of valor. As early as 1601, they had pe-
titioned the Spaniards to send them missionaries. The padres did not ar-
rive until 1614, but their early accomplishments were substantial, and
reports of the benefits they had bestowed elsewhere were convincing.

The Yaqui request was an appeal for assistance, not the supplication
of a conquered people—a distinction that was evidently apparent to the
Jesuits, for no military detachment accompanied Father Andrés Pérez de
Ribas and his aide, Father Tomás Basilio, on their entry into Yaqui country one year later. The first years of Jesuit patronage saw profound changes in Yaqui and Mayo society. By 1619 seven missionaries were at work

among the Yaqui, and virtually the entire tribe had been baptized. Over time, the Yaqui moved from their traditional rancherias—each housing up to 400 people in dome-shaped, thatch-covered dwellings—to take up residence at one of eight mission sites, whose populations ranged up to 3,000. To the south in Mayo country, seven similar missions were established along the Mayo River.

The mission villages consisted of rectangular, wattle-and-daub structures clustered in widening arcs around adobe churches. Fronting the churches were plazas, cleared of all but a few trees to accommodate religious processions. Cemeteries dotted with wooden crosses flanked each church, and nearby stood an adobe building that served as the headquarters of the town government, which consisted of Indian leaders supervised by Spaniards. At each mission site, fields radiated in strips from the river bottom lands. The Jesuits made some improvements on the simple native irrigation system, introduced oxen for plowing, and added new crops to the native roster of corn, squash, pumpkins, beans, and cotton. As among the Pima, wheat proved to be the hardiest Old World transplant, ripening luxuriously after the winter rains. Under Jesuit management, the Yaqui toiled in the fields six days a week and produced a surplus of wheat for storage or trade.

The transition was not without traumas, the most severe of which were raging epidemics that reduced the Mayo population by half within 50 years of initial Jesuit contact. For some reason, the Yaqui suffered a less severe toll. But they could not evade the moral assaults of the missionaries, who found some of their customs objectionable. Like the Pima, the Yaqui brewed alcoholic beverages for their ceremonies, a practice the priests railed against. The missionaries were similarly appalled by the Yaqui ritual of dancing around a pole adorned with the head or other body parts of a slain enemy or wrongdoer; under pressure, villagers eventually abandoned that rite in favor of a kind of Maypole dance. In addition, the priests prevailed on Yaqui men to crop their long braided hair, which traditionally reached to the waist. Henceforth, it was decreed, the locks must fall no lower than the shoulders, "as is the custom with civilized people."

Most villagers were willing to put up with such restrictions so long as the new regime offered them prosperity and security. But in the 1730s,

*Reserved for close combat, mesquite or ironwood war clubs were brutally effective. After doubling over an enemy by a jab to the stomach with the sharply pointed tip, the Pima warrior would smash the broad end of the club into his opponent's face.*

Spanish adventurers and settlers began pouring into the region, drawn by the expanding silver mines to the northwest and by the fertile pastures. The newcomers resented the fact that the best land was under mission control and reserved for Indians. Tensions escalated between Indians and the encroaching Spaniards, and between the Jesuits and civil authorities. Certain missionaries added to the friction by hiring outsiders known as "coyotes" to work in the missions, while paying the regular Indian farmers nothing. The Indians also resented the export of their surplus grain to missions in Baja California. And they seethed under the priests' habit of laying on whippings for infractions of mission rules. In 1740 Yaqui and Mayo villagers rose up in rebellion. Before the insurrection was put down, a few hundred Spaniards and perhaps 1,000 Indians had lost their lives. All the missionaries had been driven out, and entire herds of mission cattle and horses lay slaughtered in rotting, vulture-covered heaps.

Although priests returned, the missions were never quite the same. In 1771 the Spanish colonial government secularized them and transferred their administration to civil authorities. Cut loose from their ecclesiastical moorings, the mission towns moved toward a new way of life, one combining the Spanish-Catholic legacy with resurgent Indian traditions. Over the decades, the Yaqui changed the way town government operated to reflect the informal democracy of their old tribal councils. No longer could a single authority—civil, military, or religious—impose its will; the Yaqui insisted that decisions be made in open forums so that a consensus could be reached. Eventually, the Indians ceased to think of the eight towns as Spanish institutions and came to regard them as their own creations. A legend that gained wide currency among the villagers in the early 19th century traced the origin of the towns to four Yaqui prophets and a band of angels who had appeared along the river after a primordial flood. Together they had traveled from point to point along the periphery of Yaqui lands, "singing" the sacred boundaries. Later, as the prophets made their way through the sanctified territory, they experienced visions at eight spots, each of which became one of the mission towns.

The Yaqui gift for reinterpreting Spanish customs was exemplified by the annual festival known as Saint's Day, based on a Jesuit-inspired ceremony celebrating the victory of Christians over the Moors who once dominated the Iberian Peninsula. Before the fiesta, which culminated on the day honoring each town's patron saint, the entire village divided into two camps, designated the Reds and the Blues. The rival groups then competed to see which could prepare more food or stage a more compel-

*Wrapped in a cotton blanket, a Pima woman stands in her outdoor kitchen, amidst metal pots and assorted household goods. The cooking area is enclosed by an arrowwood fence that serves as a windbreak.*

ling Deer Dance—a rite designed to please the animal's spirit so that it would continue to allow itself to be hunted. On the climactic Saint's Day, the Reds played the role of the Moors and advanced from a makeshift castle in the town plaza to challenge the Christian Blues, who defended the village church. Each side was led into battle by four *fiesteros,* or "fiesta makers," who carried canes adorned with Islamic crescent moons or with Christian crosses. In the free-for-all that followed, contestants sometimes had the shirts torn from their backs. Yet the Blues inevitably prevailed and hauled their heathen opponents into the church, where they were rebaptized. Then the two sides embraced and poured out into the plaza to feast together as one, reaffirming the solidarity of a community that had happily reconciled its Christian and pagan traditions.

Tragically, the Yaqui sense of pride and self-determination conflicted sharply with the aims of the fledgling Mexican government, which marked its independence from Spain in 1821 by tightening its grip on the hinterland. Suddenly all Indian lands were subsumed within Mexican municipalities and subjected to taxation. To the Yaqui, such actions amounted to a crime against the sacred order. In 1825 authorities in Mexico City dispatched troops to the Yaqui town of Rahum to collect delinquent taxes. In outrage, a charismatic Yaqui leader named Juan Banderas, the town's former governor and captain-general, assembled a force of 2,000 Yaquis and Mayos. Banderas and his fighters ousted the Mexicans and held them off for years. At one point, the Yaqui patriot dreamed of an independent Indian state in northern Mexico. But Banderas and 1,000 of his men were defeated at Buenavista in 1833, and the captured leader was executed one year later. A Mexican general paid him tribute as a "man of genius."

The death of Banderas did not put an end to Yaqui opposition. Aided in part by the Mayo, the Yaqui spent the better part of the next half-century in armed resistance. In 1886 the Mexicans launched a determined military campaign to put down the rebellious Indians once and for all. The Mayo, who were suffering a calamitous smallpox epidemic, swiftly surrendered, with catastrophic results. Within two years, they had largely ceased to exist as a tribe, their towns depopulated by disease and slave raiding, the survivors forced into virtual servitude as laborers on Mexican haciendas.

Not the Yaqui. Those defiant people met the Mexicans head-on with a force of 4,000 warriors. Their crude arms were no match for modern weaponry. In 1886 some 200 Yaquis were slain and 2,000 more were taken prisoner. The remaining warriors fled into the mountains, where they formed guerrilla bands that continued to harry Mexican officials, with help from the 3,500 Yaquis still living in the towns along the river. In 1900 the Mexican government embarked on a harsh new campaign to drive the troublesome Indians from their land so that Mexican colonists could claim it. Within a decade, thousands of Yaqui men, women, and children had been swept into the dragnet and sold at 60 pesos a head to plantation owners as far south as the Yucatan and Oaxaca. By 1910 the Yaqui held the mournful distinction of being the most widely dispersed native people in North America.

Even so, Yaqui guerrillas continued fighting, and peace remained elusive in Sonora. At last, in 1939, Mexican president Lázaro Cárdenas held out an olive branch. He offered the Yaqui ownership of an area comprising about one-third of their original domain. Some of the Yaqui rebels

*Wearing a stuffed deer-head mask as well as rattles of dried cocoons on his ankles, a Yaqui Indian performs the ancient deer-calling dance. For centuries these desert people have evoked the spirit of the deer as a source of water, fertility, and healing.*

and exiles returned to the valley, only to find themselves facing yet another challenge, this one economic in nature. In the 1940s, the Yaqui River was dammed, and the villagers found the government managing their resources. Irrigation canals sustained the eight towns, however, and by mid-century, more than 10,000 people called them home. Against considerable odds, the Yaqui had endured.

East of the Yaqui River valley, in the rugged Sierra Madre, the Tarahumara reached their own accommodation with the hostile forces of man and nature. Long renowned for their ability to run great distances—their tribal name means "foot runners"—the Tarahumara lived in widely scattered hamlets or lone, single-family dwellings built of brush and stone. Within their mountain fastness cut by abysmal canyons descending from knife-edged ridges, life was fraught with uncertainty. Deriving sustenance from the spare soil was difficult. Each spring, the men sowed their small plots by pounding holes in the dirt with digging sticks and dropping three or four seeds into each. Until the summer rains arrived—never a surety in this region—a state of anxiety prevailed. Corn was the main crop, and a poor harvest meant months of subsisting on roots, berries, and wild plants as well as whatever game could be had. In winter, many groups moved down into the canyons to wait out the bitter cold in cliffside caves.

Like the Yaqui, the Tarahumara found much to admire and to fear in the Spaniards they first encountered. In the first decade of the 17th century, a Jesuit pioneer named Father Juan Fonte who had already won converts and introduced new agricultural techniques among the Tepehuan—the Tarahumara's traditional enemies to the south—persuaded hundreds of Tarahumaras to take up residence around a newly constructed mission church in the lowlands. In time, however, the Indians there and at other missions established in the area tired of priests hectoring them to work harder or flogging them for missing Mass. A long era of hostilities ensued, marked by the execution of Father Fonte and other men of the cloth, brutal reprisals by Spanish troops, and counterstrikes by well-organized Indian bands of up to 2,000 men. By 1698 the Spaniards had crushed active opposition in the highlands, but the Tarahumara continued to resist by eluding priests and soldiers they dared not openly defy.

As a result, the Tarahumara never incorporated Christianity into their lifestyle to the extent the Yaqui did. Over a period of time, some of them

On the Thursday before Easter Sunday, a troop of Pharisees—drums thumping and swords rattling—stride to a plaza at the pueblo church to perform the first dance of the week's ceremonies. Champions of the fearsome god Diablo, the Pharisees bare themselves to the waist and slather their limbs and faces (below) with white clay. The leader has a crown of turkey feathers.

# REVIVING THE GOD OF THE SUN

As Easter approaches in northern Mexico, musicians of the Tarahumara tribe roam the rugged footpaths of the Sierra Madre, summoning the faithful with fife and drum to the village plazas for the start of Holy Week ceremonies.

According to Tarahumara tradition, Easter is a crucial time of year. Weakened after months of winter cold, the deity Onorúame, god of the sun, is barely able to hold his evil brother, Diablo, in check. If Diablo prevails, he will destroy the earth. By taking part in the Easter ceremonies—a blend of 400-year-old Catholic liturgy and ancient Indian ritual—the Tarahumara endeavor to reinvigorate their enfeebled god. The elaborate rites pit two legions—Onorúame's Soldados and Diablo's Pharisees—against each other in a symbolic bid for control. Through the enactment of this ritual contest, the Tarahumara believe that they perpetuate harmony in their world.

*With a wave of his scarlet flag, the "waru peshi," or "important man," opens Holy Week ceremonies. Assembled in front of the church are his band of lance-bearing Soldados, soldiers in the service of Onorúame, the Tarahumara's benefactor god. Each Soldado wears a traditional loincloth and muslin poncho.*

# A CONTEST BETWEEN GOOD AND EVIL

Modeled on a Jesuit drama depicting Christ's tribulations as he bore the cross to Calvary, the Tarahumara's Easter rites involve grand processions interspersed with native dance.

Several times daily from Maundy Thursday through Good Friday, the Soldados and Pharisees convene before the church, where—after much flag waving and dancing—they enter the nave. As the Christian Mothers gather the images from the altar and exit the church, the two factions fall in behind, forming a counterclockwise procession around the churchyard.

Along the way, the celebrants pause many times to bless the images *(right)*. Later, despite taunts and sword waving by the Pharisees, the sacred portraits are returned safely to their sanctuary.

*The faithful file into the church to pay homage to the sacred images adorning the altar. Onorúame's Soldados congregate along the wall at left, keeping a wary distance from Diablo's menacing Pharisees along the right wall.*

*Kneeling before an altar portrait of Our Lady of Guadalupe, a Christian Mother ritually blesses the image before embarking on the Grand Procession (above). After crossing herself, the woman passes incense over the image nine times, then turns full circle and repeats the action two more times.*

*Pharisees perform their dance of defiance by the glow of bonfires lighted to warm the cold spring night. Afterward, they will join the Soldados, Christian Mothers, and other townspeople in a torchlight procession.*

*In accordance with a Good Friday tradition, Pharisees inspect the church roof for rotted timbers, tossing down the defective logs and replacing them with sturdy members.*

## THE DOWNFALL OF DIABLO

The cycle of promenading and dancing extends well into the night, punctuated with rousing orations. By evening on Good Friday, however, the ritual antics have grown more confrontational: Using straw and Western-style clothing, the Pharisees make a Judas figure to parade about provocatively. On Holy Saturday, they lash their effigy to a pole and dance at his feet *(below)*.

The three-day contest climaxes after Saturday's Grand Procession. In a tussle between opposing factions, the Soldados capture Judas and burn his straw stuffing. The forces of renewal triumphant, the rest of Holy Saturday is devoted to wrestling matches and a beer fest. Sunday is a day of rest.

*On the afternoon of Holy Saturday, the Pharisees mass on the plaza adjoining the church, where they have erected a straw figure of Judas. Skipping and whooping, Diablo's servants dance about the pole in mock homage to Christ's betrayer.*

*Two young Tarahumara women compete in a footrace, a traditional sport for male and female alike. As part of the game, these racers carry sticks for scooping up small fiber hoops and tossing them ahead on the trail. Special rattling belts around their waists sound the rhythm of the runners' strides.*

came to identify the God of the Spaniards with their traditional Great Spirit, known as Onorúame, and many professed belief in a rival deity called Diablo—Spanish for "devil." But a sizable portion of the tribe remained outside the Christian fold. Even today the Tarahumara are divided into two groups: the unconverted Gentiles and the Bautizados, or baptized ones, who mark the Christian holy days with dances and rituals that owe a large debt to pre-Christian ceremonies.

Whatever their spiritual differences may be, Gentiles and Bautizados alike take part in household ceremonies such as the beer fests known as *tesgüinadas,* which occur as often as 60 times a year. Each fest lasts up to two days and typically involves a small circle of family and neighbors who have gathered to help their host harvest a crop or perform some other task requiring cooperative effort. Once the project is completed, the laborers receive their due—typically a fresh brew of milky, bitter stout drawn from fermented corn mash. Since every drop of beer must be consumed on such occasions, all the guests—men and women alike—have an opportunity to attain what the revelers call a "beautiful intoxication," accompanied by the shedding of blissful tears.

Aside from giving the normally stoic Tarahumara an emotional outlet, the gatherings provide these isolated people with a forum for settling local disputes, arranging marriages, and making business deals. The Tarahumara drink almost exclusively within the institutionalized setting of the tesgüinada, and lead an otherwise sober and vigorous life. Long-distance running remains their greatest diversion. Young women sometimes take part in races of up to four miles, and the top male athletes compete over distances of more than 100 miles. To compound the challenge, runners must advance a wooden ball with their feet for the entire length of the course. Betting on these foot-throwing games, as the Tarahumara call them, is an avid pastime for those on the sidelines.

Aided by their historic isolation, the Tarahumara remain one of the most populous native peoples in North America, numbering about 50,000. Although they have adopted some things from the outside world, they still speak their own language, make most of their tools, grow much of their food, and live dispersed throughout the rugged country that offered them refuge from intruders.

Far from the Tarahumara homeland, Yuman-speaking Indians of northwestern Arizona have long pursued a similar round of foraging, farming, and simple ceremonial fellowship in a setting nearly as rugged as the Si-

erra Madre. Known collectively as the *Pai,* or the "People," these Upland Yumans have closely identified themselves with sacred places in the stunning geographical tableau extending from the south rim of the Grand Canyon to the northern fringes of the Gila River basin. One such group, the Havasupai, or "people of the blue-green water," took their name from the turquoise waters of Cataract Creek, which empties into the Colorado River in the Grand Canyon. Each summer, the Havasupai diverted the creek's flow at the base of the gorge to cultivate narrow plots of corn, beans, and squash—and more recently, sunflowers and fruit. As autumn approached, the people climbed the steep walls of the ravine with their storage baskets and camped in log-and-pole lodges on the forested plateau, where they collected firewood, gathered nuts, and hunted game to see their households through the hard winter.

The kindred Hualapai, whose ancestral territory bordered that of the Havasupai on the west, likewise attached great significance to the waters that nourished them. Indeed, legends of the Hualapai trace their very origins to the canyon of the Colorado, where the Great Spirit conceived a plan to transform the tall canes that grew by the riverbank into the first humans. To accomplish the task, it was said, the Great Spirit ordered the fabled trickster and wonder-worker Coyote to cut a multitude of stalks—enough to foster a vast population—and lay them out with their tops facing eastward. Coyote was then instructed to wait quietly through the night for the sun to rise on a new race. But Coyote could not contain his excitement, and his howls pierced the darkness, so angering the Great Spirit that he decided to change only a few stalks into people. Thus the Hualapai, like the Havasupai, remained a sparse tribe, numbering perhaps a thousand souls, who moved back and forth between their low-lying plots and their hunting grounds on the high plateau.

For another Upland Yuman group, the Yavapai, whose domain lay to the south of the Hualapai and Havasupai, life originated in the Red Rock Mountains of Sedona. There, in a cliffside cave, Yavapai legends attest, First Woman was embraced by Sun and Cloud and gave birth to the human race. Most of her descendants dispersed, but the Yavapai remained at the center of the world, drawing inspiration from the cave, where members of the tribe still pray for friends in need. Compared to their northern neighbors, the Yavapai came to control a wide territory and proliferated, numbering in the thousands in historical times. Their combativeness when roused made them feared by the Havasupai and Hualapai, and by the white frontiersmen who entered the area in the 19th century.

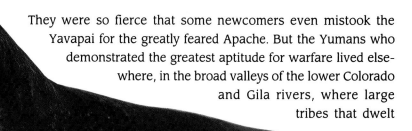

They were so fierce that some newcomers even mistook the Yavapai for the greatly feared Apache. But the Yumans who demonstrated the greatest aptitude for warfare lived elsewhere, in the broad valleys of the lower Colorado and Gila rivers, where large tribes that dwelt

*This miniature Quechan clay pipe, which was molded in the shape of a human face and painted with traditional Quechan facial designs, was probably made for trade.*

in uneasy propinquity competed for dominance. Like their linguistic cousins in the uplands, these River Yumans had inhabited the region for many generations before the arrival of the first white men. Their ancestors may have been foragers from what is now southern California, who drifted eastward across the desert to plant seeds on the fertile banks of the two silt-laden rivers. In time, three main tribes emerged in that area: the Quechan (sometimes referred to as the Yuma), who dominated the junction of the Colorado and the Gila; the Mohave, who lived upstream along the Colorado near the desert that bears the tribe's name; and a coalition of peoples who came together in the early 19th century under the title of the Maricopa and lived along the Gila, near villages of the Pima.

From late fall until the early spring, the River Yumans congregated in settlements situated on high ground, safely above the flood plains. Dominating these villages were large lodges set into the ground and covered with earth to protect occupants against the cold. In severe weather, up to 100 Yumans, young and old, male and female, might crowd into such abodes. But as soon as conditions permitted, they would return to flimsier single-family huts nearby. In the growing season, the people moved to similar brush shelters located near the fields, where they cultivated abundant crops of corn, beans, and pumpkins.

Farming supplied only about half the food that was required by the people. The remainder came from fishing, hunting, and gathering. The women spent a great deal of their time collecting mesquite pods, screw beans, and other wild foods. If they came upon the nest of a squirrel or other hoarding animal, they appropriated its stash. These gathering forays might last for days at a time and range some 50 miles from the river. Men went along for protection and to hunt rabbits and other game. In times of drought, they scrambled after rats, mice, lizards, and snakes.

The diet obviously provided more than adequate nutrition, for the River Yumans were a muscular and fit people. The Spaniards who first encountered the Quechan during the 16th century reported to their compatriots that a healthy man could heft a log too heavy for several white men and swim the Colorado River with a large basket of goods. The People were hardy, too. One Spaniard marveled that the men went around unclothed and the women wore bark skirts even in winter, occasionally alleviating the cold with firebrands, "which the natives carry in their hands, warming the pit of the stomach."

In their outlook on life, the River Yumans were fatalistic without being passive or gloomy. They believed that nature, like the rivers they relied on, had an inexorable rhythm and flow that could not be altered but could be interpreted so that people would act in a manner that harmonized with nature's design. Thus, the Yumans did not stage elaborate rituals designed to bring the rivers to flood stage or the crops to fruition. Instead, they gave thanks for the bounty when it matured with songs, dances, or lovemaking. And throughout the year, they sought counsel from their dreams, which they saw as powerful and prophetic signals from the spirit world. The Maricopa believed that a person who dreamed of an eagle would be able to sing songs that cured people. One Maricopa related such a dream: "Eagle is high in the sky. He takes the dreamer up there and shows him the various places and mountains, naming them for him. Eagle shows him the whole valley and tells him how to go about his work curing people." The Mohave, for their part, believed that bad dreaming could make people sick, and that only a shaman guided by good dreams could restore them to health.

The River Yumans looked for leadership to those of their fellow tribesmen who had the most powerful dreams. According to the Mohave, such visions first came to the chosen ones when they were in the womb. The dreams would be forgotten in childhood, only to recur in adolescence. Eventually, the dreamers would sing of their visions and be recognized as leaders. Among the Quechan peoples, tribal elders met to select as chief the man who they thought had the best dreams, but the selection did not confer permanent authority on the leader. His influence lasted only as long as events bore out the truth of his visions. If his advice led the tribe astray, people concluded that he had lost the power, and they turned to other dreamers for guidance.

Good dreaming was vital to success in the warfare that so absorbed the River Yumans. Economic factors undoubtedly helped predispose these peoples to conflict. The amount of arable farmland along the flood plains was limited, and competition for the best plots increased tensions between groups. In the long run, however, the frequent warfare in the area had less to do with material gain than with personal and tribal prestige. Only in battle could an individual prove his physical and spiritual strength, and bring honor to his people.

A small group of warriors might embark on a raid with minimal guidance, but a larger venture culminating in a pitched battle required the active participation of a war leader—usually someone other than the tribal chief—who galvanized his followers both with his strength and fearlessness and with his dreams. One Maricopa war leader dreamed of clouds of flies battling each other in midair. By reading their movements, he learned how to deal with the enemy. In battle, one or two standard-bearers carrying feathered pikes led the way; they were expected to press forward at all costs. Next came the champions, the outstanding warriors of the tribe, followed by as many as 200 braves.

The timing and location of a battle and the choice of weapons were often arranged in advance; rival groups might decide to employ only clubs, or perhaps both clubs and knives, during the conflict. At the designated hour, the opposing sides approached each other, halted, and faced off. The champions then strode forward, trading insults and menacing gestures before closing with their counterparts in one-on-one combat. Then the bulk of the braves joined the fray, fighting furiously until one side was thoroughly beaten.

The scalps that the victors collected conferred spiritual benefits. Scalps were powerful; only those who had dreamed the requisite dreams were allowed to take them. The Maricopa believed that if a warrior untouched by dream power claimed a scalp, the dead enemy would grin—and the would-be scalper had reason to fear for his life. Not every fallen enemy was scalped. After the battle, warriors scouted the field for victims with long, fine hair. Once such a man was found, the scalp taker ritually broke the warrior's neck across his knee. Then, taking his knife, he cut across the bridge of the nose, under the eyes, below the ears, and around the back of the neck. This done, he pulled the scalp free.

Special rituals sanctified the scalps. The Maricopa, for example, believed that anything associated with the enemy was polluted and dangerous; hence, all those who had slain an enemy or taken scalps or captives were required to undergo a lengthy purification process. After battle, the

*A Hopi woman carefully picks a bunch of sharp-edged yucca leaves to be dried in the desert sun and later woven into baskets. Although yucca can be harvested all year, winter is the best time to gather the spines because they are most flexible then.*

*A Navajo medicine man makes suds with yucca roots. Traditionally, yucca soap has been used for both sacred and secular purposes, including washing the hair of Hopi brides and cleaning Navajo rugs.*

# THE VERSATILE YUCCA

For hundreds of years, Indians have found the succulent yucca to be the most versatile plant in the desert, a provider of everything from sugar and soap to ceremonial materials. From the ancient Anasazi to modern Hopi basket makers, people of the Southwest have extracted sinewy fibers (often with their teeth) from spiny-tipped yucca leaves to weave into sandals, nets, mats, baskets, and brushes. Some varieties of the wild shrub bear a banana-shaped fruit that pregnant women once ate in order to ensure an easy delivery; today the Navajo and Pueblo peoples still cook the fruit for use as a food sweetener. And the roots of the plant, also known as soapweed, provide the region's only natural soap.

*Native peoples of the Southwest today continue to weave with yucca, producing items such as this coiled Hopi basket (left). The plaited yucca ring rest (above), used to keep pots steady when they are carried on top of the head, is a design that has remained largely unchanged for centuries.*

warriors were quarantined in brush huts that had been erected outside the settlement. There, they fasted for 16 days, rising each dawn to bathe. The scalpers carried their trophies with them at all times, washing the scalps when they bathed, and sleeping with them on their chests. At dawn following the 16th night, the warriors returned to their homes. For four days, they remained at the back of their huts, facing the sunset. On the morning of the fifth day, they emerged fully cleansed.

The custodian of scalps, always an elderly former warrior, gathered the new scalps and mounted them on deerskin hoops atop long poles. Now the community engaged in a day of dancing and a night of singing—the scalp dance celebration. At the conclusion of the festivities, the custodian removed the trophies from their hoops and placed them in a large clay pot, which contained all the scalps the tribe had collected in the past. According to tradition, the scalp keeper listened for omens as the scalps talked together in the pot. If they were laughing, he knew that some evil awaited his people; if they wept, it meant that a future enemy was doomed.

As befit people who made such a ritual of warfare, the River Yumans greeted death with great ceremony. Funerals were typically held within a day or so of death. Amid much wailing, people bathed and groomed the corpse and placed it on a pyre of timbers stuffed with dried arrowweed. As the pyre was lit, grievers added to the conflagration the dead person's belongings—clothing, sandals, blankets—anything that would burn. If the deceased was a mounted warrior, as some Yuman fighting men were by the 19th century, his horse, daubed with war paint and tethered nearby, was killed so that it could carry the man and his goods to the land of the dead. After cremation, relatives dug a hole in the floor of the house and buried any

belongings that had not been burned or given away. The family then torched the dwelling. If the dead was head of a household, his crops were distributed to friends, his granary burned, and his fields left fallow for up to two years. The family moved to an entirely new location, for they believed that if any trace of the deceased remained, the spirit would return to haunt the dreams of the living. After four days of mourning, the relatives were admonished to stop thinking of the departed, and the dead person was no longer referred to by name.

*Quechan men were particularly proud of their long hair, often wearing it in mud-plastered rolls that fell below the waist (left), or coiled up inside a woven turban to display its bulk (above).*

Once the spirit of the deceased had safely departed, however, a ceremony of remembrance might be held, often on the anniversary of the death. Dancing, singing, and other activities alternated with gift giving, as the family offered baskets of food, equipment, and clothing to their guests, who then might indulge in gambling or athletic competitions before staging a mock battle. The ceremony culminated with the cremation of a figure that had been dressed and painted to look like the departed.

Schooled in the art of war and unflinching in the face of death, the River Yumans defied all efforts of the Spaniards to subdue them. The early contacts between the two groups were sporadic and relatively peaceful. But the Quechan, in particular, had something the Spaniards coveted—control of the ford later known as Yuma Crossing. There, just south of its juncture with the Gila, the Colorado squeezed between two rocky hills, narrowing almost to a stream. Except in times of flood, the river was easily passable at that point—but nowhere else, which gave the Quechan power over who came and went across the Colorado. Beginning in 1771, the Spaniards undertook a series of expeditions to the area, with the ultimate object of wresting control of the crossing from the Quechan and establishing a fort at the site that would secure it for men and supplies traveling overland from the Mexican heartland to the burgeoning network of Spanish missions and garrisons being set up in Baja and Alta California.

In 1774 a party of 34 Spaniards headed by Captain Juan Bautista de Anza and Father Francisco Garcés made their way down the Gila to the Colorado, where they met with a Quechan leader who was accompanied by 60 gaudily bedecked warriors. The chief, known as Olleyquotequiebe—or Wheezy One—wore a small blue-green stone suspended from his nose, while the noses of the others were adorned with rings, feathers, palm sprigs, or bones. Painted from head to toe with red hematite, charcoal, and other pigments, these Indians presented a formidable sight and filled the newcomers with foreboding.

As it turned out, the Spaniards need not have worried, for in the coming days, the Quechan extended every courtesy to their guests. In February Anza ceremoniously appointed Olleyquotequiebe, thereafter known as Salvador Palma, governor of the Quechan, and presented to him a red sash and a Spanish coin. Afterward, in an effort to ensure Palma's continued cooperation, Anza outfitted the Quechan leader in a splendid uniform with a yellow-fronted jacket, a blue cape decorated with gold trim, and a black velvet cap adorned with paste jewels. Anza then informed Palma that, as governor of the Quechan, he was subject to the king of Spain, who had dominion over his people and all their lands. Palma paid the pronouncement little attention. Such a declaration held no meaning for him, or for any other Quechan.

As was the case with other leaders in the area, Palma derived power from dreams, and for the time being, his dreams pleased his people greatly. The Spaniards invited Palma to Mexico City, where he was baptized and showered with gifts. His hosts spoke glowingly of the benefits that would flow from having a Spanish mission at Yuma Crossing.

Palma returned to his people with promises that they would receive further gifts from the Spaniards. Moreover, to please his patrons, the Quechan leader renounced all but one of his several wives, and showed such devotion to his new faith that Father Garcés was moved to remark: "Captain Palma would put to the blush many veteran Christians, imitating the most devout in making the sign of the cross, beating the breast, and other demonstrations of devotion."

In 1777 King Charles III of Spain authorized the establishment of a mission and military garrison in Quechan territory. Such an incursion might have been less objectionable to the Quechan if the gifts they had been promised were forthcoming. But two years passed without the arrival of any presents, and the Quechan increasingly suspected Palma of bad dreaming. Palma made three trips to Sonora to inquire about the situation. Finally, in August 1779, Garcés returned to Quechan territory, but he brought no gifts. Another priest and a dozen soldiers followed in October, and they too were empty-handed. By November the disillusioned Quechan had stripped Palma of his role as tribal leader.

A few score Spaniards now lived among the Quechan. The outlanders brought practically no supplies with them and depended on the Quechan to furnish them with food. That was strain enough. A crop failure in the fall of 1780 exacerbated the situation. Then, in December, the Spaniards arrived in force—another 21 soldiers escorting 107 women and children, with precious few provisions to support them. The soldiers and settlers already on site began building two small outposts, one atop a rocky prominence to the west of Yuma Crossing, the other 12 miles downstream. As winter gave way to spring and the Spaniards made no move to plant their own crops, the Quechan grew more restless. The Spaniards had their own complaints. Father Garcés's initial enthusiasm turned to anger as the Quechan resisted his Christian teachings. "They are the most crude people on this frontier," he wrote, "and much too stupid to be attracted to spiritual things."

Worse was to come. In June 1781, a large Spanish expedition on its way to California passed through Yuma Crossing, leaving behind a dozen surly soldiers to mind several hundred farm animals. While their commander permitted the livestock to ravage the Indians' crops, the men tried to force themselves on Quechan women. As if this were not enough, the Quechan learned from the Spaniards' Indian interpreters that the soldiers were talking of killing them.

The Quechan decided to strike first. On the morning of July 17, Quechan warriors mounted simultaneous attacks on both outposts, killing 55 men, including Father Garcés and three other priests, and taking 76 Spaniards captive, most of them women and children. During the course of the fighting, Palma was seen destroying Christian icons at the mission church. His dreams may have inspired the uprising, for the Quechan soon restored him to a position of leadership.

Three months later, a detachment of nearly 100 Spanish soldiers appeared, having been assigned the mission of rescuing the captives and executing the Quechan leaders. Palma had little interest in feeding useless prisoners, and he returned many of them as soon as the Spaniards arrived. Yet try as they might, the soldiers could not seize the Quechan leaders and ultimately departed in frustration. Other Spanish expeditions launched periodic offensives over the course of the next year, but they failed to regain control of Yuma Crossing. The Quechan were once again undisputed masters of their realm.

The ouster of the Spaniards brought no peace to the region, for the recent struggles had only increased tensions among the River Yumans. The Quechan had a particular score to settle. During the battles of 1781, a small group of Yumans to the north of them, known as the Halchidhoma, had joined with the Spaniards in the hope of defeating their age-old Quechan rivals. Once the Spaniards were gone from the area, the Quechan combined with the Mohave and turned on the Halchidhoma, who eventually fled to join other refugees along the Gila—the people who became known as the Maricopa. This realignment set the stage for a series of costly battles, with the Quechan and Mohave on one side and the

# IN PRAISE OF THE ALL-GIVING TURTLE

The Seri Indians, who make their home on the desert coast of the Gulf of California in northwestern Mexico, have for many centuries drawn their existence from the bountiful waters, and in return, they sing the praises of the marine creatures on which their lives depend. Most of all, the Seri extol the virtues of the sea turtle, that generous provider of meat and shell. So venerable is the sea turtle in the eyes of the Seri that they credit the animal with participating in the creation of the world.

The tribe honors this legendary creature on the rare occasions when they are able to catch a Pacific leatherback turtle, a leviathan known to weigh as much as 1,500 pounds and to grow as long as eight feet. After harpooning the behemoth, hunters tow it ashore, supposedly at the request of the creature, and keep it alive in the shade of a traditional brush hut. They then paint its carapace and flippers with designs that they believe connote power. A four-day celebration ensues, similar to a girl's puberty ceremony, during which the Seri honor the giant with song, dance, and gambling games.

Much more common than the Pacific leatherback, the smaller green sea turtle once made up as much as 25 percent of the Seri diet. In addition to the meat, the turtles' shells provided a building material used to construct everything from children's sleds to pottery kilns to houses. Harpooning a green turtle was considered such an important skill that young men were not considered fit to marry until they proved that they had mastered the technique. Commercial hunting of the turtles became a major source of revenue for the Seri during the mid-20th century, but in recent years, overharvesting has led to a greatly diminished turtle population and a consequent loss of income for the tribe.

*An artist who visited the Seri depicts their world, complete with brush huts and reed grass boats, as a huge turtle. One version of the Seri creation story describes how the ancient giant sea turtle brought back earth from the depths of the ocean.*

*Descended from a long line of woodcarvers, the Seri produce crafts, such as this ironwood porpoise, that are reflections of their coastal heritage.*

*The decorations painted on the face of a young girl for her puberty ceremony are similar to those worn by the giant turtle, considered to be a maiden.*

*A ceremonial dancer performs for a captured leatherback during a 1981 turtle fiesta near Punta Sargento in Sonora, Mexico. The shell of the turtle is painted with dot and line designs, and green branches of the sacred elephant tree are scattered around the animal as ritual offerings.*

*After the festival, Seri celebrants drag the giant leatherback to the ocean to set it free. In times past, the Seri frequently ate the revered guest at the end of the fiesta.*

Maricopa and their newfound allies, the neighboring Pima, on the other.

Such internecine strife weakened the River Yumans at a time when they faced a formidable new challenge. In 1848 the United States took control of much of the area from Mexico, leaving only those Indians east of the Colorado and south of the Gila under Mexican jurisdiction. The Gadsden Purchase six years later placed almost all the Yumans under federal control. The first inkling most Yumans had of the new order came in 1849, when thousands of gold seekers bound for California surged past Yuma Crossing, acting as if the land belonged to them. With them came hordes of livestock that stomped and chewed their way through the fields. Overwhelmed by the onslaught, the Indians could only stand by—and look for ways to hurry the intruders along. Shrewdly, the Quechan began to ferry the forty-niners across the Colorado for a fee. The ferry business soon made them prosperous, but it also led to their undoing. Anglo-American entrepreneurs set up ferry businesses of their own that cut into Indian profits, and established outposts on Quechan lands. The Quechan drove off some of the interlopers, only to find new ones in their place.

It was not long before the Ferry Wars, as the clashes were called, incited anti-Quechan passions as far west as Los Angeles. In the fall of 1850, John Morehead, a belligerent lawyer and politician, invaded Quechan territory with a makeshift militia of 125 men. The vigilantes wrecked several of the Quechan ferries and laid waste their crops. The tribe's response was swift and characteristic. Warriors descended in force on Morehead's crew and drove them into a fort that had been established by a white ferry operator. Afterward, the vigilantes were permitted by the Quechan to return home—relieved "to get back with a whole scalp," as one riverman put it.

The matter might have ended there. But frustrated citizens succeeded in propelling the U.S. Army into action. In short order, three companies of infantrymen were dispatched to Quechan lands, where they launched a series of attacks that destroyed Indian villages and crops. Although the Quechan fought back valiantly, they were no match for the well-armed troops. By October 1852, the United States government had assumed control of Yuma Crossing.

Elsewhere, other Yuman tribes suffered similar reverses. In 1858 the Mohave attacked a wagon train bound for California, killing 18 Ameri-

*Clay dolls fashioned by the Quechan mimic traditional tribal dress and the practices of body painting and tattooing. The female doll carries a baby in the bustle of her skirt.*

cans and driving off 600 head of cattle. United States cavalrymen armed with rifles struck back. In a one-sided battle with Mohave warriors wielding only their bows and arrows and clubs, the soldiers killed more than half of the Mohave war party and scattered the remainder. Some months later, a contingent of 500 soldiers arrived to build a fort on prime Mohave bottom land and lay down the conditions for peace. The Mohave were compelled to surrender their tribal chief and eight other leaders—five of whom were later slain during what the army called an attempt to escape. The defeat devastated the Mohave, and never again did they challenge the government.

In 1863 the Upland Yumans began to feel the pressure from newcomers in their territory. A gold strike in Prescott, Arizona, brought prospectors flooding in, while cattlemen appropriated rangelands and water holes, often at gunpoint. The Yavapai—few of whom had firearms—put up with such insults for a while, but soon they began to fight back. In 1871 the government ordered all of them confined to a reservation and stipulated that any who refused to be relocated should be treated as hostile. A year later in Salt River Canyon, a large band of Yavapai men, women, and children hoping to elude detention followed the example of their ancestors in times of stress and sought refuge in a cave. Federal troops discovered the hiding place and took the Indians by storm. The site of the one-sided battle became known as Skeleton Cave.

By the mid-1880s, all the Yuman peoples had been restricted to reservations that comprised only a fraction of their ancestral lands. No longer could the People range far and wide in pursuit of game or wild growth to supplement the harvest, and many of them took day jobs off the reservations in order to support their families. Some tried to put the tribal past behind them, as they would a loved one who had died. But the memory of the ancestors and their struggle lived on, even if people did not speak their names. Their collective spirit endured and bound communities together, as expressed in a Quechan mourning oration: "All the sick hearts of our people will change. This day is passing away now; we are all together now; we will think well now that we are all together in this place. People, it will be well. This day is going. We commune with one another. I will find our strength. I will find our good. On that I rely."

PEOPLE OF THE DESERT

# 3

# IN THE REALM OF THE APACHE AND NAVAJO

Barely a thousand years ago, small bands of nomads—driven perhaps by hunger or hostilities—abandoned their lands in the wind-swept reaches of the far Northwest to seek a more plentiful realm. They had embarked on a journey that would carry them more than 2,000 miles. Traveling along the edge of the great Rocky Mountains, the immigrants made their way southward over a period of time that spanned several centuries. When at last they reached what is today the American Southwest, they halted; here they would live, staking out vast tracts where they hunted game and gathered wild plants.

*A young Western Apache woman draws water in a basket sealed with piñon pitch to render it leakproof. The nomadic Apache carried much of what they gathered or owned in lightweight woven baskets. Bucket-shaped burden baskets such as those lashed to the horses transported grain and firewood as well as personal goods from one campsite to another.*

The newcomers were the last native people to settle in this region of broad, semiarid plains broken by mountains, mesas, and canyons. In the icy reaches of their old homeland, the nomads had stalked caribou, moose, and bear and trapped fish in the frigid lakes and streams. As befit a roving people, their shelters were simple constructions—a few slender poles draped with branches or hides—and probably clustered in small family enclaves. Laboring to eke out a living, these northern people had little time for ceremony, and their religion was an unelaborate one based on controlling the forces of nature and curing the ill through the efforts of shamans, who received their power from dreams and visions.

During the long trek, little happened to change such customs. The immigrants arrived piecemeal in the Southwest beginning perhaps around AD 1500, with their culture intact. After following the great bison herds down the High Plains, most of the nomads spread out across the open country east of the Rio Grande, but at least one group made its way into the more broken terrain of the Four Corners region. They spoke dialects of a common language stock, called Athapaskan, forms of which are still spoken today in parts of Alaska, Canada, and the American Northwest. They called themselves *Tinneh,* "the People," but in time they would be known by names given to them by others—Apache and Navajo.

The travelers must have been astonished by the sights that greeted them. Across the sunbaked landscape of present-day Colorado, New Mexico, and Arizona, the nomads encountered large communities of Pueblo Indians living in sprawling adobe dwellings, some of which housed hundreds of people. Rather than depend solely on the vagaries of nature for food, these villagers had joined seed and soil, and broad fields of corn, cotton, beans, and squash surrounded their settlements. While the men tended the crops, their wives ground corn, wove mats and baskets, and molded clay pots with striking red, white, and black markings. Perhaps most astonishing of all, in the eyes of the immigrants, were the pageants that pueblo dwellers performed as a means of communicating with the legion of spirit beings who inhabited their complex universe.

For decades the nomads roamed over the Southwest, some fanning out across the southern reaches of the Plains, others making their way into southern New Mexico and eastern Arizona. The foreigners accustomed themselves to the new land, with its rough-hewn beauty, and they quickly learned how to tap its resources. Soon they had all but surrounded the Pueblo Indians, some of whom—probably the Zuni—labeled the newcomers apacu, meaning "stranger" or "enemy." The Spaniards would transform this word into Apache.

Bit by bit, the nomads adopted some of the ways of their neighbors. Those groups who roved closest to the Pueblo settlements learned to farm, weave, and make pottery. They also incorporated into their own rituals some of what they had witnessed in the village plazas—elaborately costumed and masked dancers, for instance, who represented the spirits. Bands that ranged toward the east, on the other hand, took up buffalo hunting and built tipis, like the Indians of the Great Plains.

A legend about the early years in the Southwest tells how the People learned to grow corn. According to the tale, a young man hunting for wild game happened upon an ice-covered lake. At a hole in the ice, he found a magical ladder down which he climbed, descending through the water to the bottom of the lake. There he gazed in wonder at fields of colored corn stretching to the horizon in all directions—white corn in the east, blue in the south, yellow in the west, and black in the north. At the margins of the field stood four large dwellings, in matching hues. The hunter visited these houses, and at each one, the inhabitants gave him two beautiful women to wed and four ears of corn. Then they instructed him in the ceremonies required to grow the grain. Gathering up the ears of corn, the hunter ascended the ladder, returned to his people, and taught them what

An Apache girl carries water in a pitched basket, or "tuus," suspended from a long tumpline across the top of her head. The sturdy containers, often colored with red ocher or crushed juniper leaves beneath their waterproof pine-pitch coating, were plugged with leaves, bark, or wads of yucca root.

he had learned. Eventually, he went back to the magical lake to live among the people of his wives. Perhaps in a manner much like this, a nomadic hunter visited a Pueblo village and returned to his own people with the knowledge of agriculture.

The Spaniards invaded the Southwest in the mid-16th century, disturbing a way of life that had existed for centuries. Francisco Vásquez de Coronado was on a mission for the viceroy of Mexico, searching for seven golden cities described in an ancient legend. The explorer and his troops never found the fabled kingdom, only adobe pueblos and some scattered bands of the nomadic hunters. "They travel like Arabs, with their tents and troops of dogs loaded with poles," one member of Coronado's party wrote of the nomads. Coronado himself found them a "gentle people, faithful in their friendships." For their part, the People were probably as astonished at the spectacle of the Spaniards, with their cavalcades of horses, sheep, and cattle, as their ancestors had been when they encountered the well-organized Pueblo villages.

In the early years, the Apache and the Navajo traded amicably with the Spaniards, much as they had with the Pueblo peoples. Intrigued by the Spaniards' possessions, the Indians willingly exchanged wild animal skins for trinkets, tools, and livestock. The People were particularly fond of the taste of horse meat, and it was not long before they realized how much easier mounts would make their hunting and foraging. The period of harmony was short-lived, however. Hungry for cheap labor, Spanish raiding parties began attacking the Indian camps, seizing prisoners to use as slaves. The People fought back, and stepped up their raids on other tribes, mostly Pueblos, that the Spaniards had drawn into the colonial fold. By the middle of the 17th century, intermittent but vicious warfare had become commonplace in the region.

At the time of the Spanish invasion, the nomads claimed an area stretching several hundred miles from present-day western Oklahoma to eastern Arizona. Like any people spread out over a vast and variable landscape, they gradually splintered into distinct groups, which the Spaniards began to distinguish with separate names. During the years of warfare, the cultural rifts between the nomadic bands deepened, and by 1700, there were seven tribes, scattered in a broad swath of land.

Spread out along the northern borders of New Mexico and Arizona were the Apaches de Nabajo—later shortened to Navajo—who developed

*A Navajo silversmith identified as Slim, Maker of Silver, displays a large concha belt and other examples of his art for a studio photographer in 1885. Taught to work silver by the Mexicans in the late 1860s, the Navajo were soon trading finished goods, following a bartering tradition that stretched back to their first contacts with the Spaniards.*

*A mounted Navajo woman tends her flock of sheep on New Mexico's Ramah Reservation. Since their introduction by the Spaniards, horses and sheep have been indispensable to the Navajo; in times past, wealth was measured in terms of the number of horses a man owned or the size of a woman's flock.*

a far different way of life than the other groups. Far to the east, mingling with the Plains Indians, were the Lipan and Kiowa Apache. The Jicarilla and Mescalero claimed large areas east of the Rio Grande; the Chiricahua and Western Apache lay west of the river, in the south of Arizona and New Mexico. While each tribe developed a regional cast, the six Apache groups still retained a similar means of subsistence and a shared religion. True to their hunter-gatherer heritage, they followed the seasons, breaking camp in early spring to forage for plants, hunting in the fall, and only settling into semipermanent dwellings during the cold winter months. Those who lived closest to the Pueblos dabbled in agriculture, using domestic crops to supplement their stores of food.

The Western Apache, for example, made their winter camps in the valleys of the Salt, Black, and Gila rivers, in southeastern Arizona. When the grass turned green and yellow flowers bloomed on the mesquite, they packed their goods and walked northward, into the mountains, where they farmed for a brief period, tilling the soil in long, narrow plots. Here, alongside the cool mountain streams, Apache men cleared shallow ditches to channel water to the fields. They pried rocks loose with sticks, heating the larger boulders with fire and dousing them with cold water to shatter them for easier removal. Wielding pointed sticks, the women loosened the warming earth and punched shallow holes into which they dropped the seeds of corn, beans, and squash. The Western Apache valued diligence highly, and group leaders would often encourage their people to work hard, raise large crops of corn, and help one another.

During April or May, when the first seedlings sprouted, the focus of life changed. Leaving children and elders behind to tend the fields, men and women descended to lower elevations to gather mescal cactus, a staple of the Western Apache diet. Although the community made use of nearly every part of the mescal plant, the large crowns—some weighing as much as 20 pounds—were the most useful, yielding a source of food that lasted many months. Once a promising stand of mescal had been located, the women would uproot the plants and harvest the crowns, using special knives to peel away the foliage. Meanwhile, the men dug large pit ovens, some as many as 12 feet across and four feet deep. In these hollows, the mescal crowns were roasted whole for two days; then they were pounded into thin cakes, dried, and rolled into bundles for transport back to the campsite. While the crowns were cooking, men and women abstained from sexual relations—failure to do so, the Apache believed, would result in an underdone and inedible product.

In June, gathering parties left once again to forage for saguaro, prickly pear, and cholla cactus; in midsummer there were mesquite beans, yucca fruit, and acorns to be gathered. Only in October, when the ripe crops beckoned, did the Western Apache pause in their migrations—and then only briefly, for hunting was best in late fall. While women combed the slopes for piñon nuts and juniper berries, men stalked deer, antelope, and mountain sheep. In general, boys had to be nearly grown before they were allowed to hunt large game. According to one Western Apache, a young boy's heart "would not be strong enough to stand it; it could make him ill or even kill him."

Apache hunters relied almost exclusively on their powerful bows, which were often backed or wrapped with deer sinew to increase the weapons' killing power. Arrows were crafted of reed and the tips sometimes treated with special poisons. The toxins used by the Western Apache were concocted from various blends of blood and venom aged in putrefying animal entrails. The resulting potions were thought to be so lethal that should a treated arrow merely graze a deer hide, the animal would die. Apache hunters usually skinned and butchered their prey on the spot, carrying the meat back to camp in bundles tied with yucca cord. There it was preserved by smoking or drying. Just as important as the meat were the hides, especially buckskins, which were scraped, cleaned, and softened and later worked into clothing, containers, and a host of other items. Among most groups, generosity was a valued trait, and an Apache hunter shared his bounty not only with his relatives but also with other families, giving special care to those less fortunate than himself. "Our custom is to be generous about the meat and hide," said a Mescalero elder who lived into the 20th century.

With the first chill of winter, families gathered up their bounty and went back to their lowland camps. Here they lived in shelters known as wickiups, which were usually erected by the women. Apache homes resembled those of their Athapaskan forebears—conic dwellings

*Red suede fringe trims a contemporary Western Apache burden basket woven in the classic shape. By the 1880s, many Apache baskets were being made for a commercial market, sold to occupying troops, incoming settlers, and eventually to tourists arriving on the newly built railroads.*

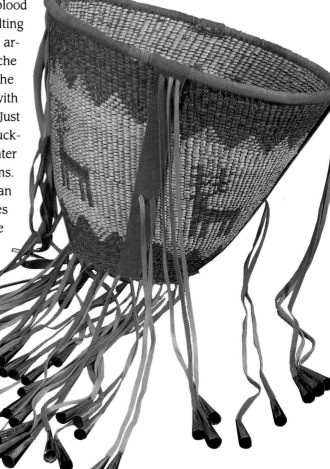

*Snugly strapped into its wooden cradle-board, an Apache baby smiles contentedly beneath a canopy adorned with protective charms. Cradleboards were highly versatile: They could be propped up or laid flat, carried on a mother's back, or hung from the side of a horse, familiarizing infants early on with the constant motion of Apache life.*

with a framework of slim, sturdy tree limbs covered with whatever material was at hand, often the leaves of the yucca plant, which grew abundantly in the region. The Apache had an abiding fear of the dead, who they believed could return as ghosts to haunt and disturb their relatives and friends. When members of the group died, therefore, their wickiups and all the possessions inside were destroyed.

When an Apache couple married, the new husband typically joined his wife's family—and, from that point on, exhibited a healthy deference to his new in-laws. Depending on the group, custom dictated that an Apache man never speak directly to his in-laws, or at the extreme, never allow himself to be in the presence of his wife's mother. Perhaps a dozen extended families banded together in an encampment for protection and to share the daily routine and the traditional ceremonial activities. These local groups chose chieftains, male or female, who most epitomized the Apache ideals of industry, generosity, and patience.

During the lean winter months, Apache men raided and hunted while the women occupied themselves with tanning hides, stitching clothing, and weaving baskets, a skill for which they are famous even today. Crafted from plant parts—usually yucca, sumac, and mulberry—and often embellished with strands dyed red, blue, and yellow, Apache baskets are finely woven, with a simple utilitarian elegance. Traditionally, three types were produced—round, shallow trays used for parching seeds and sifting grain; tall, flat-bottomed burden baskets for transporting and storing goods; and amphora-like vessels for holding water and tiswin, a mild beer the Apache brew from freshly sprouted corn. Apache women prided themselves on these watertight containers, which they sealed by smearing melted pitch from the piñon tree over the interior of a woven basket. Sometimes the outside too was covered with pitch as well as decorated with various dyes. The technique was ingenious—when a woman's water basket began to leak, she simply reheated the pitch and smoothed it over the cracks. Basket making itself was so intimately connected with wom-

en that baskets were taboo on hunts—it was felt that their presence, like the presence of a woman herself, would bring the hunters ill fortune.

With the arrival of the Europeans, the Apache entered a new era—one in which horses played a major role. The Indians first saw these animals when Coronado crossed their lands in the early 1540s; within 50 years, the Apache were supplementing their diets with horseflesh and hunting and fighting on horseback. They became expert riders and raiders. In the late 19th century, an American general assigned to subdue the Indians deemed the Apache the "finest light cavalry the world has seen."

Horses were particularly valued by the eastern Apache peoples, who hunted large herds of buffalo that migrated across the Great Plains. On horseback, it was many times easier to pursue and kill the huge beasts. Perhaps because of this, the Jicarilla Apache considered horses to be a gift from the supernatural powers, requiring extreme respect at all times. The Jicarilla sang special songs in honor of the horse, and handled with

*This Western Apache wickiup, a traditional design, was assembled from grasses tied to a frame of bent saplings. Buffalo-hunting Apache, such as the Mescalero and Jicarilla, adopted the Plains tipi as their shelter.*

special care the ropes, saddles, and other gear associated with horses.

Acquiring horses—and other livestock—became a major goal of Apache raids. For centuries the Apache had taken whatever they needed from the earth; raiding was for them a natural extension of their hunting and gathering tradition, with human settlements simply another resource for food and supplies. Most looting forays took place in winter, when food ran low and hunger threatened. During this time of want, a leader would call upon men to volunteer for an assault on a Spanish settlement or another Indian community. A raiding party would form, consisting of a handful of men willing to brave the ordeal. A group of Chiricahua elders interviewed in the 1930s remembered raids that they had witnessed as young boys during the previous century. "They went on raids because they were in need," one of the old men recalled. "As few as five or six would be in the party. About 10 is the most that would go. Usually, but not always, one who had power connected with war was along. It was just according to how it happened."

The Apache conducted their attacks with cunning and stealth. Mounted on horses, the raiding party proceeded slowly. When the men entered enemy territory, they used great caution, speaking only in a special code. "When they are on a stock raid, they don't want to be seen," one Chiricahua remembered. "They sneak around. They are careful; they avoid meeting troops or taking life." The attack usually occurred in the early morning hours, when the victims were least likely to be on guard; some Apaches timed their raids for several days before the full moon, when there would be just the right amount of light. On the fringes of the enemy settlement, two or three men would break away from the rest and noiselessly approach the herd on foot. They maneuvered the animals into the open, where the rest of the party surrounded them and drove them off. The two groups reunited on the fly, and everyone drove the animals home at breakneck speed, often going without sleep for several days.

By the mid-18th century, the Apache were assaulting the Spaniards with devastating frequency, plundering their scattered ranches and farms for horses, cattle, and other goods. The Spaniards retaliated by establishing military strongholds and launching repeated campaigns against the raiders. Late in the century, the Mescalero Apache were attacked by Spanish forces in what is today the Big Bend region of Texas, as well as along the Rio Grande and the Pecos River. Retreating to mountain sanctuaries, the Mescalero proved an elusive foe. The exasperated Spaniards set Indian against Indian, bribing the Lipan and Mescalero to attack each other and withhold aid to any other tribe. When this tactic also proved ineffective, the Spanish authorities settled the Mescalero in restricted areas, only to find themselves under attack from the new encampments.

Beginning in 1786, the Spaniards tried yet another approach to dealing with the Apache. First the colonial overlords made a show of force with their soldiers, while encouraging the Indians to seek peace. Then they settled the more compliant Apache around Spanish forts and gave them food, clothing, firearms, and liquor in return for an agreement that the Indians would put an end to the raiding. The guns were inferior, and as the Spaniards intended, the alcohol weakened the Apache society and subdued the raiding urges. This insidious policy produced a period of relative calm that lasted about 35 years, until 1821, when Mexico gained its independence from Spain. The fledgling country could not afford to buy off the Apache, who again took up raiding as a way of life.

Despite acquiring a taste for certain Spanish commodities, the Apache continued to follow their traditional ways, honoring the spirits that they believed to be innate in all natural phenomena. For the Apache, as for all Native Americans, spiritual life was inseparable from the daily routine. Whether gathering wild fruit, planting a field, or embarking on a hunt, the Apache observed innumerable rituals and taboos to honor and influence the powers that animated their world. In this way, they might ward off disaster and secure the success of their endeavors. Great care was taken when preparing the mescal plant, for instance. At sunrise, a person deemed by his fellow tribesmen to be lucky offered a prayer to the sun—the source of all fire—asking that the mescal cook properly. One Western Apache prayer praised the heavenly inferno, the "fire which never goes out, Black Sun, his fire." After suitable tribute had been offered, the wood inside the firepit was ignited in ritual succession—first the east side, then the south, west, and north.

Similar care was taken in agricultural tasks. While hoeing and irrigating, the Apache prayed and addressed their crops, which were thought to contain some of the supernatural power of the universe. They feared lightning and made it the object of many taboos—corn was never sown in a field that had been struck, for example, nor was a person who had been struck allowed to plant seeds of any sort. In fields where crops were planted, Apache shamans placed prayer feathers to lure rainfall and, at the same time, stave off floods. Among the Jicarilla, the new moon was

*A young Chiricahua Indian draws his bow across a one-stringed fiddle fashioned from a hollowed section of an agave plant. Apache fiddles were probably inspired by the Spaniards' musical instruments.*

honored with a special rain ceremony—each man who headed a family group puffed smoke onto four turkey feathers, one at each corner of his family's field. Because the Jicarilla linked the moon to water, this ritual was thought to cause the skies to open.

Ceremonies to ensure good fortune in hunting—and in raiding and war—were essential elements of Apache life. Before beginning a hunt, an Apache man purified himself with sweat baths and abstained from eating certain foods—hunters from one band of Western Apache avoided meat and salt, and ate only mescal whenever possible. The night before the hunt, the men sang, prayed, and offered sacrifices to the spirits. Hunters continued to invoke the powers while on the chase—an Apache who spotted a deer track might offer puffs of tobacco smoke to the sun before stalking his quarry. Even the kill was often performed in a ritualized manner, and many Apache hunters avoided wolves, coyotes, and foxes, ani-

*An Apache game of hoop-and-pole begins with two men poised to hurl slender willow sticks after a rolling hoop. Usually accompanied by heavy wagering, the contest was scored according to a complex point system based on the final position of the hoop relative to marks or notches on the poles.*

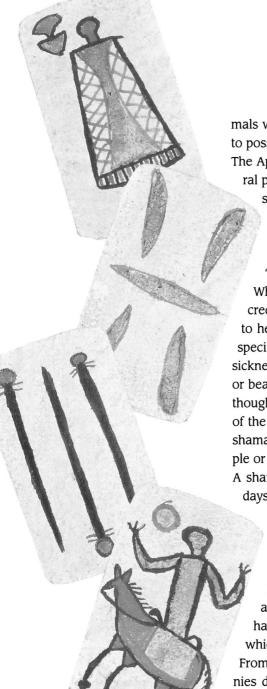

*Painted rawhide playing cards are cut with rounded corners to about the size of the printed Spanish and Mexican decks on which they were modeled. Apache men and women were enthusiastic cardplayers, and gambling on games was a favorite pastime.*

mals whose meat was taboo. The mountain lion, however, was thought to possess special power, and its meat was offered to shamans only.

The Apache continued to depend on shamans as vehicles for supernatural power. These men and women held influential positions in Apache society. Often selected for their task early in life, most shamans attained power through dreamlike visions, which came unbidden, appearing in the form of animals or other natural phenomena. "Some say that the earth talks to them," explained a Chiricahua. "Some say the wind has life. Some say the mountains."

Whatever form the vision took, it instructed the chosen person in sacred songs and prayers to be used during a particular ritual, most often to heal the ill or the troubled. Each ceremony was designed to cure a specific illness—the Jicarilla holiness rite, for example, guarded against sickness believed to be caused by the malevolent influence of wind, fire, or bears. The ceremonies served a larger purpose as well, for they were thought to restore health and well-being not only to the patient but to all of the community members who participated in the rite. Furthermore, a shaman could also use his power for other purposes—to locate lost people or objects, to weaken an enemy, or to control the weather.

A shaman's work was arduous. Healing ceremonies usually lasted four days and nights (four being a sacred number), during which time the shaman might sing as many as 80 chants, each containing some 30 verses. At the end of the rite, the shaman might produce an evil charm that he claimed to have sucked from the patient's body—this, it was believed, had caused the illness. During one Mescalero ritual, for example, the shaman displayed a three-inch, arrow-shaped bone, colored blue and tipped with red. Four human hairs were wound around the object. The shaman said that the bone, which he had taken from the patient's head, was a witch's weapon.

From birth until death, the Apache also observed a number of ceremonies designed to ensure long life, good fortune, and well-being. These rites generally did not require the services of a shaman; an individual who had learned the appropriate songs and rituals at the feet of a tribal elder was considered capable of overseeing them. Among some Apache groups, for example, there were specific ceremonies for placing infants in cradleboards (where they would spend most of their daytime hours), others for babies' first steps or first haircuts.

Boys were carefully trained for raiding or making war. During an adolescent's first four expeditions, he was expected to remain serious and

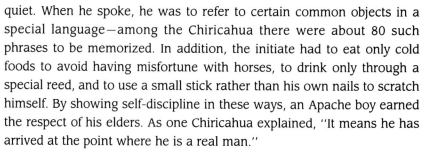

*Strips of leather hang from the edge of a Mescalero buffalo-hide war shield. Believed to have protective powers, shields were so valuable they were passed on through the generations.*

quiet. When he spoke, he was to refer to certain common objects in a special language—among the Chiricahua there were about 80 such phrases to be memorized. In addition, the initiate had to eat only cold foods to avoid having misfortune with horses, to drink only through a special reed, and to use a small stick rather than his own nails to scratch himself. By showing self-discipline in these ways, an Apache boy earned the respect of his elders. As one Chiricahua explained, "It means he has arrived at the point where he is a real man."

*An Apache buckskin war cap trimmed in beadwork bears a metal concha centered on a horned figure that provides power to the wearer. Only seasoned warriors wore the war caps, which were highly individualized in decoration and design.*

Women have traditionally exercised considerable influence in Apache life, and an intricate ceremony evolved to initiate young girls into adulthood. During the four-day event, a girl entering puberty took on the role of Changing Woman, a key figure in Apache legend symbolizing the earth and femininity. Preparation for the ceremony might begin a year in advance: A female sponsor and a male singer were asked to serve, and a buckskin costume—dyed yellow to represent pollen, a fertility symbol—was created for the girl. The event, attended by numerous friends and relatives, was held at a special campground, where a ceremonial tipi or other structure was erected. At sunrise on the first day, the young girl underwent a ritual that transformed her into the personification of Changing Woman. First she washed her hair in yucca-root soap. Then, facing east, she allowed her sponsor to mark her face with pollen and arrange her hair and clothes. Now she was referred to only as Changing Woman and was believed to have healing powers for the next four days.

Throughout the ceremony, the girl was expected to conduct herself with dignity and to observe certain taboos. Like a boy on his first raids, she was permitted to drink only through a reed. People attending the ceremony spent the days socializing and feasting. At night, masked men, representing spirits, appeared and danced to sacred songs. At a certain point, the singer

# BESEECHING THE MOUNTAIN SPIRITS

The Mescalero Apache tell a tale about two ancient warriors who were grievously wounded in battle and forced to hide from their enemies in a deep cave. One of the men was blind, the other crippled, and it seemed they were doomed until a group of mysterious dancers suddenly appeared, filling the cavern with warmth and light. The warriors were cured and led to safety—a miracle that ever since has been celebrated by the Mescalero Indians in ritual dances that are held to banish sickness and evil.

The story of the rescued warriors is but one of many legends related to the mountain spirits, or *gaan,* which the Apache believe were once sent to earth as emissaries from the Supreme Being. Charged with teaching people to live reverent lives, the gaan eventually returned to their mountain homes. But before leaving, they taught the Apache people how to summon them in the form of masked dancers.

Like the Hopi kachinas, gaan are personified by men who don ritual masks in order to take on the powers of the spirits. During rituals that employ dance, prayer, and song, the masked men bring these powers to bear on such critical enterprises as healing, averting anticipated disasters, or ushering young girls into womanhood in the female puberty ceremony.

*In this 20th-century painting, Chiricahua gaan dancers perform the Mountain Dance under the supervision of a shaman, who is shown standing at the rear of the circle with his arms upraised.*

*An early 1900s Western Apache gaan mask has a crown of split yucca stakes attached to a U-shaped frame beneath the cloth hood. Hoods, formerly made of buckskin, are pierced with small mouth and eyeholes, which wearers often tear wider during the heat of a dance.*

*Modern gaan head-
dresses are com-
monly fashioned
from thin wooden
slats painted with
enamels. Masks are
taken apart and
hidden after a dance
to prevent them
from being worn by
people who are not
dancers. It is said
that any nondancer
who puts on a gaan
mask will eventu-
ally go mad.*

drew the girl aside and performed chants just for her, meant to prepare her for a long and fertile life. At the conclusion of one song, an Apache explained: "This song is about flowers. We are taking this girl through a beautiful life, past flowers, through seasons with their fruits." Upon sunrise of the fifth day, the ceremony came to a conclusion. As the first rays shone on the girl, the singer marked her with the symbol of the sun—painted on his left palm—and tied a piece of shell or turquoise in her hair. From this point on, she was considered a woman.

With some modification, these rituals are still observed by many Apache peoples. The ceremony is, perhaps, a symbol of the enduring nature of Apache life. Much else has changed, irrevocably altered by the past 150 years. Herded onto reservations in the mid-19th century, when Mexico ceded the Southwest to the United States, the Apache have had to relinquish many of their age-old hunting and gathering traditions. Settled on remnants of the vast lands they had roved for centuries, they were left with neither the space nor the resources to pursue their chosen way of life. As one Apache of the time described a reservation in Arizona: "Take stones and ashes and thorns, with some scorpions and rattlesnakes thrown in, dump the outfit on stones, heat the stones red hot, set the United States Army after the Apache, and you have San Carlos."

For the Apache, the latter part of the 19th century was a nightmare of bloody battles, broken treaties, and forced migrations to one undesirable patch of land or another. The Chiricahua, who fought American troops for 40 years, were forced onto tracts in Florida, Alabama, and Oklahoma before finally being allowed to settle with the Mescalero on a reservation in southern New Mexico, where they—and the Mescalero—lived for 50 years under the threat of eviction. At one point, a United States senator proposed that their homeland be made into a national park.

Other Apache tribes were similarly hounded. Under such relentless pressure, they have outwardly conformed to modern ways. No longer do the Apache live in scattered encampments—most build homes near towns, where they have access to schools, hospitals, and stores. Hunting animals and gathering wild plants—once the mainstay of Apache life—are pastimes today. But the spell of the land has never been broken—the forested peaks where mountain streams watered Apache fields and the broad plateaus where they hunted game still stretch as far as the eye can see. And in each Apache individual there remains a memory of the past. Families are still close. Healing ceremonies are still performed. And in countless smaller moments, Apache traditions live on.

One group of the People became so distinct from the rest that in time they were no longer called Apache. These were the Navajo, or, as they still call themselves, *Diné,* "the People." In the early days, they settled in the country where the ancient Anasazi had built their magnificent stone dwellings, largely in north-central New Mexico. For the Navajo today, this ancient homeland of mesa and canyon is *Diné Tah,* "Among the People," the sacred place where their ancestors dwelt and the home of the spirits who created earth and the human race.

Like their Apache kin, the Navajo live in a world animated by supernatural powers that must be constantly heeded through daily rituals and taboos. The Navajo also conduct complex ceremonies, some lasting more than a week. Performed by sacred singers known as *ha'athali,* these rituals employ chants and sand paintings to recount the intricate legends of the People. They remind the Navajo of the correct relationship of the human race to the earth and its creatures. By observing the pertinent rituals, and behaving properly in their daily lives, the Navajo seek to maintain balance in the universe, a state of ideal harmony they call *hózhǫ*

Most Navajo ceremonies seek to relieve pain or cure illness. They treat sickness thought to arise from lightning or thunder, for example, with the Shootingway; for maladies caused by snakes, the ha'athali perform the Beautyway. The Navajo ceremony most often performed, however, is the Blessingway, which marks important events in life and seeks to secure good fortune and good health for the celebrants. When a child is born, when a man and woman marry, when a new home is completed, the Blessingway chants are performed. These holy songs and prayers tell the story of the Navajo creation. The ceremony reminds the People that spirits reside in all natural things, and according to one observer, it provides a "fine result in any phase of the life cycle, from birth to old age."

According to the sacred songs, the earth's creatures originated in a series of underworlds, where they lived in darkness. These animals and spirits journeyed to the earth's surface through a hollow reed, which expanded as their population swelled. As they ascended, the creatures left behind confusion, uncertainty, and error. At last their journey brought them to the current world, where harmony and happiness were eventually attained—the qualities of hózhǫ the Navajo strive to maintain today.

In the beginning, however, the primordial ancestors of the Navajo underwent much travail. The earliest people, the Navajo say, were First Man and First Woman, who lived near Huerfano Mountain in the Diné

*A collection of Nightway masks lies spread out in front of a Navajo singer, or medicine man. Traditionally made from the hides of deer that had been run down and ritually strangled, masks were trimmed with a variety of materials, including hair, feathers, and dyed sheep's fleece. Between ceremonies, they were stored flat in sacred bundles along with other Nightway paraphernalia.*

Tah. Their initial task was to bring light to the universe. From a large turquoise disk, the couple created the sun; then they sculpted the moon from a piece of rock crystal. As darkness gave way to the first dawn, a baby was born on Gobernador Knob. First Man and First Woman found the infant, nestled in a cradleboard of rainbows and sunrays. With help from the spirits—known among the Navajo as Holy People—the couple raised the child on pollen and dew. She grew up to be Changing Woman, the most beautiful maiden who ever lived. It was she who created the Navajo people, from sacred cornmeal and scrapings from her own skin. Changing Woman also bore two sons, Monster Slayer and Child Born of Water. In ancient times, these heroes roamed the earth, ridding it of monsters and making it safe for humans and animals. Only then, according to the Navajo legend, did the creatures of the earth dwell in peace and harmony.

As did the Apache, the Navajo lived in small enclaves composed of extended families. Although they grew crops, the clans still moved often, seeking out the wild plants and game that continued to make up a large portion of their diet. They erected simple homes, called hogans, on frameworks of poles covered with a thick layer of earth—the clay soil of the Southwest was ideal for this purpose. More substantial than Apache wickiups, hogans were typically used through successive seasonal growing cycles, especially as the Navajo became more tied to farming.

*Snake-shaped prayer sticks (below) and a prayer board with a picture of a snake-handling figure (right) were part of the ritual equipment made by medicine man Little Singer for use in the Windway ceremony. Gastrointestinal ailments, thought to be caused by snakes, are among the illnesses that Windway practitioners aim to cure.*

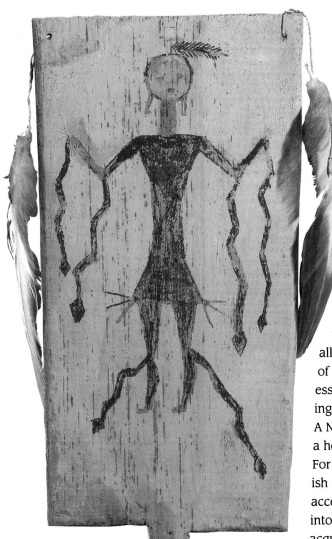

Despite their simplicity, hogans are also considered sacred dwellings. The Navajo believe the first hogan was made by the Holy People, the spirits who roamed the earth in the early days, and they take care to preserve the structure's holiness. The entrance always faces east, toward the rising sun. When a hogan is completed, it is consecrated with corn pollen, "that this place will be happy." The hogan would cease to be sanctified when its owner died, however. The Navajo retained the Apache distaste for death and all associated with it, and they usually destroyed a dead person's dwelling so that the ghost of the deceased would not come back to haunt them. So essential are hogans to Navajo ritual that they are still being built today, often adjacent to contemporary dwellings. A Navajo who lives in a modern house is likely to return to a hogan to celebrate a sacred ceremony.

For many years, the Navajo remained untouched by Spanish influence. The invaders were busy subduing the more accessible Pueblo Indians, and they rarely sent expeditions into the Navajo heartland. But by the 1650s, the Navajo had acquired horses, and a taste for getting even more. Through the rest of the century, the Indians staged raids to secure more mounts and other livestock imported by the Spaniards. The Spaniards retaliated. Greedy for laborers, they would periodically swoop down on Navajo settlements and make off with a grim haul of slaves.

One Navajo, a small boy in the mid-17th century, lived to tell the story of Spanish cruelty. On a late summer day in 1659, Spanish troops attacked a group of Navajos harvesting corn in the San Juan River valley. The boy's aunt and uncle were killed in the fighting, the family's hogans burned, their crops destroyed. Then, after a hungry winter, the Spaniards struck again. First, under guise of peace negotiations, they lured the boy's father and other Navajo leaders to a church in a nearby pueblo, where they stabbed them to death. Then the troops mounted horses and galloped north to the Navajo enclave, where they seized the boy. He was sold as a slave and spent many years in bondage in Mexico. Upon the death of his owner, the boy, now grown, obtained his freedom and became a silver miner. Finally, he learned that the Spaniards had left Navajo country, driven out by Pueblo Indians—who, in 1680, launched a massive

The so-called forked-pole, or conic, hogan (above) was the earliest form of Navajo dwelling. At right, a woman weaves a rug in a modern, spacious hogan with straight log walls and a cast-iron stove instead of the traditional open firepit. According to legend, the Holy People built the first hogans of abalone, turquoise, and obsidian as examples of ideal dwellings.

uprising with support by the Navajo. Worn and toothless, the man, now about 40 years old, began the long walk home.

He arrived just before the Spaniards returned to wreak a campaign of vengeance and terror against the Pueblo Indians. In mortal fear, many of the village dwellers sought refuge with the Navajo—the Jemez Pueblo, for instance, sent their young women north to the Diné Tah, begging their neighbors to "find husbands for our girls, so that if our pueblo is destroyed, the Jemez blood will be preserved." So closely did the Pueblo Indians live with the Navajo in the following years that the descendants of the women refugees became the first members of the Coyote Pass Clan, whose name is taken from the Navajo word for Jemez. Of the 60 or more extant Navajo clans, around one-third have a Pueblo origin.

For nearly a century, the Pueblo and Navajo peoples lived side by side in the Navajo heartland. Ruins of the straight-walled stone houses of the Pueblos have been found scattered among remnants of the Navajo hogans. It was during this period that the culture of the Navajo people was transformed by the influences that they absorbed from their neighbors. From the Pueblos, they learned the techniques of weaving wool and other handicrafts. They picked up invaluable agricultural skills and were exposed to a rich Pueblo religious and ceremonial life. The Navajo embraced a number of Pueblo spiritual practices, including some of their legends and the ritualistic sand painting, but they rejected elements that seemed to conflict with their ancestral values. They shied away from the seasonal community ceremonies so prominent in the lives of their neighbors. And they never adopted the Pueblos' kiva for rituals; although for a time they built stone structures called pueblitos, in the end they retained their hogans both as dwellings and as ceremonial centers.

It was from the Spaniards (and often indirectly through the Pueblos) that the Navajo acquired animals—horses, sheep, goats, and cattle—and the techniques for raising and enlarging their herds. From the Spaniards, the Pueblos had learned to shift the animals between valley and plateau, seeking fresh pasture and water. Soon the Navajo began to do the same. But while Spanish and Pueblo ranchers sent only a few herders to accompany the animals, the Navajo—perhaps because of their nomadic tradition—broke camp with their herd. It was not unusual for a sheepherding family to move three or more times a year.

This way of life continued into the early 20th century. A Navajo born in 1919, for example, recalled his family's annual migrations. Each summer, after planting their crops, the family packed their wagon and donkey and journeyed three days with their stock to higher ground. Along the way, they hunted rabbit and picked berries. At harvesttime, some members returned to the lowland fields while others remained with the animals. In the fall, the young boys picked piñon nuts, moving from place to place and living in brush shelters. "We traveled so much in those days," one old Navajo recalled. "We did not worry about our hogans and blankets and valuable things. When we came back, they would all be there."

Among the Navajo, the women owned and tended the sheep, while the horses belonged to the men, who bartered goods and staged raids to increase their herds. As time passed, the People grew wealthy. More and more, they measured success by the size of their herds. Livestock became so important that new Navajo legends sprang up tracing the domestic animals back to primordial times. According to one such story, the sun itself once possessed a flock of sheep in four colors; while deliberating on the pattern of the stars, the gods first arrayed them on a sheepskin.

During the years that the Pueblo Indians lived among them, the Navajo also learned to weave fine woolen cloth. Once again, however, the People credit the gods rather than humans. They were taught to weave, legend says, by Spider Woman, who first practiced the art in ancient times, weaving a raft to rescue earth's creatures from a flood. In fact, the ancestors of the Navajo did engage in a rudimentary sort of weaving; they plaited yucca leaves and mountain grasses to make a crude fabric for mats, blankets, and leggings. But it was only after sharing their homeland with the Pueblo Indians that the Navajo began crafting the tightly woven, boldly patterned cloth that has earned them worldwide acclaim. Right from the start, the quality of Navajo weaving was remarkable—in 1795 a Spanish governor noted that they worked their wool "with more delicacy and taste" than European craftsmen.

While men were the weavers among the Pueblos, weaving was a female art in Navajo households, which added to women's already considerable status. In times of want, weaving often kept Navajo families alive. Women sheared the sheep, and spun and dyed the wool, obtaining the soft hues from wild plants. They created yellow dye, for instance, by cooking the flowers of rabbitweed—a plant with a slender stalk and clusters of golden blossoms—for six hours, then mixing in a paste made from native alum. The wool was then boiled in the dye until it reached the desired color—anywhere from bright yellow to deep gold.

Seated on a sheepskin outside her hogan, singing and praying, a Navajo woman might spend more than 200 hours completing a small blanket.

# THE LEGACY OF SPIDER WOMAN

According to Navajo legend, Spider Woman taught artisans of the tribe to weave in ancient times on a fantastic loom composed of sunrays and lightning bolts. The Navajo hold that this holy person still dwells in a sacred lair in Arizona's Canyon de Chelly where her spirit works through individual weavers, gently guiding their hands. So steadfastly do the Navajo believe in the powers of Spider Woman that parents rub the hands of their infant daughters with spider webs to ensure that her gift is passed on.

The development of Navajo weaving has been strongly influenced by Pueblo Indians as well as by Spanish colonists and Anglo-American traders. In the mid-17th century, Pueblo refugees fleeing Spanish rule in the Rio Grande Valley brought the vertical loom and more efficient techniques of weaving to Navajo country. Although Pueblo weavers were traditionally male, Navajo women took over the art and began to incorporate novel geometric designs adapted from Spanish textiles. Their boldly patterned blankets were used as everything from bedrolls to dresses.

By the 1880s, an improved transportation system had brought the Navajo into frequent contact with white traders, who encouraged new styles aimed at a market beyond the reservation. Navajo women wove the new motifs into their blankets, and their artistry gained them fame far beyond the desert Southwest.

*In a photograph taken around 1850, a Navajo woman shapes an intricate pattern using yarn hand spun from sheep's wool. Navajo artisans working today take advantage of manufactured yarn (bottom).*

# TRADITIONAL DESIGNS

Before the middle of the 19th century, Navajo women relied primarily on wool in undyed shades of white, gray, and brown, which they obtained from their own flocks. In time, some of the weavers introduced muted colors into their blankets with dyes extracted from sagebrush or juniper berries, or indigo dissolved in fermented urine.

When explorers and traders brought a European flannel cloth called bayeta to Navajo country, artisans unraveled its crimson threads to incorporate into their creations. Two basic styles of woven goods prevailed: the striped shoulder blanket worn like a shawl in the Pueblo tradition, and the longer serape, an adaptation from the Spaniards.

*The so-called Chief Blanket evolved from a simple pattern of contrasting stripes (left) to a more complex series of crosses on stripes (above). Despite its name, the Chief Blanket could be worn by any member of the tribe.*

*Woven of wool and bayeta, a Navajo serape from the 1860s takes both its name and its interlocking diamond pattern from garments that were worn by Spanish colonists in the Rio Grande Valley.*

# WEAVING IN NEW DIRECTIONS

When the Santa Fe Railroad crossed the southern edge of the Navajo reservation in 1882, it spawned trading posts along the route that supplied weavers with brightly colored, chemically dyed yarn, giving rise to a host of vibrant new designs. Especially popular was the four-ply Germantown yarn, spun in the Pennsylvania town of the same name. In addition to bringing an improved array of yarns to choose from, the trading posts provided new outlets for the weavers. Enterprising traders relayed the preferences of Anglo customers for large, heavyweight rugs rather than traditional blankets.

*Bright interlocking sawteeth, woven primarily with chemically dyed yarn, resemble waves of heat rising from the desert surface in this 1890 blanket, which early traders labeled an "eye dazzler."*

*A Navajo weaver displays a rug for the merchant Juan Lorenzo Hubbell (seated) in front of his trading post in Ganado, Arizona.*

*This blanket woven in the 1880s depicts the new world that was encroaching on the Navajo, with its two-story houses and locomotives. In that era, a few artisans shifted from abstract patterns to pictorial designs featuring everything from letters of the alphabet to the American flag.*

*Around 1900, white traders intent on expanding the market for Navajo rugs introduced oriental motifs to artisans of the tribe. Weavers responded with designs such as this 1915 rug with a central medallion and narrow border.*

At first, the patterns were simple: natural brown and white stripes with, perhaps, a strand of indigo blue woven in for color. Before long, however, Navajo women began experimenting with dyes and patterns, weaving in yellow, green, red, and blue designs. Over time, the patterns became more elaborate—simple linear motifs gave way to large, interlocking diamonds and wide, zigzagging bands. Many early Navajo blankets have strands of a crimson hue that could not be produced with native dyes—to obtain these brilliant threads, Navajo women unraveled Spanish bayeta, a soft woolen cloth for which they bartered. Traditionally, the designs were never made with a bordered edge—Navajo women always left a gap through which the spirits that occupied the cloth might escape.

Although the Navajo soon began to trade their textiles for other necessities, they also used them in their daily lives, for blankets, beneath saddles, as clothing. Navajo women wore dresses fashioned from two woven blankets stitched together along the sides. Atop their buckskin breeches, Navajo men donned woven shirts and slung shoulder blankets. And to shield themselves from wind, cold, and blowing sand, both sexes wore colorful woolen shawls called serapes, in which they carried everything from firewood to babies.

Toward the close of the 18th century, the Navajo were a changed people—more numerous, more adept, more wealthy. While Navajo men continued to hunt and Navajo women continued to gather wild plants, the People were now proficient in both agriculture and livestock raising. In learning to weave, they had acquired a craft that would serve them well in years to come. Most impressive, though, were their vast livestock holdings. A Spanish report from 1785 tallied about 700 Navajo families, each one with four or five people, and recorded more than 1,000 horses, 700 female sheep, and 40 cows, with additional bulls and calves. All the livestock, the Spanish observer noted, were "looked after with the greatest care and diligence for their increase."

As Navajo population swelled and livestock numbers grew, the People began to spread out, mostly to the west and the south, away from the ancestral

*Small charms like the twig "spirit catcher" were hung in hogans to fend off the ghosts known as "chinde." The charms were sometimes hung in groups of four, a spiritually significant number for the Navajo as well as for other tribes.*

heartland. They called the region to which they migrated the "land between four mountains," for the peaks that stood in each of the cardinal directions. To the north is Hesperus Peak in Colorado's La Plata Mountains, and to the south, Mount Taylor in New Mexico. The San Francisco Peaks in Arizona guard the west, Colorado's Blanca Peak the east. Each promontory, they say, is crowned with a sacred jewel, stone, or feather.

According to Navajo legend, these hallowed mountains were fashioned by the spirits from soil they gathered in the ancient underworld. Between the mountains stretches a ruggedly beautiful landscape—vast highlands cut by cinnamon-red canyons and enclosed by the sky's blue dome. Water here is scarce, but in springtime, a thousand bright flowers speckle the countryside. Here, Changing Woman was found and the evil monsters that plagued humankind were slain—their carcasses, the Navajo say, form some of the spectacular features of the landscape. "These mountains and the land between them are the only things that keep us strong," an elderly Navajo storyteller explained in the early 1980s.

Across the land between four mountains, the Navajo ranged in the 18th and early 19th centuries, no longer on foot, but on horseback. Like the Apache, they often raided Spanish holdings to increase their herds. Small groups of young men rode through the countryside, plundering settlements as far south as Chihuahua. "There were good, large ranches in Mexico, where we always got our sheep," one old Navajo recalled.

Navajo men carefully prepared themselves for these raids, for only if certain rituals and taboos were observed could a mission be successful. Well in advance of a foray, the group's leader sought the special powers he would need by hiring a medicine man to teach him the Enemyway, a chant based on an ancient raid. By learning the ritual, the leader prepared himself to "step into the shoes of Monster Slayer, step into the shoes of him who lures the enemy to death." Then, for three days before the raid— odd numbers being significant in warlike ventures—all members of the raiding party purified themselves through sweat baths, singing, and prayer. Afterward, they donned shirts made from three or four layers of buckskin—a kind of armor—and dipped their arrows into a magic poison made from the charred remains of a tree struck by lightning.

Once under way, the men ate only certain foods, slept in prescribed positions, and used only approved words when speaking to one another. They were ever alert to signs of ill fortune. If an owl hooted or a coyote crossed their path—animals generally feared among the Navajo—the men turned back, for their mission was doomed to failure. On the other hand, should the raiding party encounter horses or sheep, they had every reason to believe their venture would succeed. If all signs pointed to victory, the men proceeded. The night before the event, they painted their bodies with pictures of bear tracks and snakes to gain additional power and courage. At dawn, they swooped down on the flock that had been targeted for plunder, sometimes taking hundreds of sheep in a single outing.

The era of raids—indeed, the period of peak Navajo strength—ended in the early 1860s. Yet another country had gained control of the Southwest, and with all the zeal of a growing nation, the United States set out to end the raiding—and crush the Indians. A U.S. Army officer, General James A. Carleton, took on the task of pacifying New Mexico. On September 6, 1863, in the midst of the Civil War, he wrote to his commander in Washington describing his strategy for subduing the Navajo: "The purpose now is never to relax the application of force with a people that can no more be trusted than you can trust the wolves that run through their mountains; to gather them together, little by little, onto a reservation, away from the haunts, and hills, and hiding places of their country."

To carry out this campaign, Carleton appointed a seasoned frontiersman, Colonel Kit Carson, who commanded a regiment of volunteers. Carson's mission was to round up as many of the Navajo Indians as possible and move them to the plains of eastern New Mexico. Those who resisted the forced move were to be taken prisoner—or killed if necessary. To hasten the process, Carson encouraged other tribes, the Ute among them, to attack and harass the hapless Navajo peoples.

The area chosen for the new settlement was called the Bosque Redondo—Round Grove—for the solitary patch of green it boasted, a thicket of cottonwood trees. Aside from this small oasis, the reservation was empty wasteland. Utterly lacking in natural shelter, it was as unlike the folded Navajo landscape as the white man's ways were alien to Indian. On this barren ground, according to the army's plan, the Navajo would become year-round farmers, and the size of their herds, which were their tokens of prosperity and well-being, was severely restricted. Meanwhile, Navajo crops were to be burned, Navajo livestock seized or slaughtered.

On a bitterly cold day in January 1864, some 200 Navajos left their home in Canyon de Chelly to begin the long trek toward Fort Sumner, the American stronghold in the Bosque Redondo. Over the next months, hundreds more surrendered to federal troops or were taken prisoner. In large convoys, they trekked east—1,400 in February, 2,500 in March. The journey, mostly on foot over several hundred miles of rugged terrain, was

*A sand painting created as part of a Bless-ingway ceremony to ensure a good corn crop depicts in colored sand the deity Changing Woman, who is standing on a blue cross that represents Mother Earth, from whom the cornstalks grow. The foot-steps indicate Changing Woman's ascent from the underworld; the rainbow bars sur-rounding her represent Father Sky. Bless-ingway rites, held to invoke positive influ-ences rather than to cure illness, are the ceremonial linchpin of Navajo religion, em-bodying the striving for the order and har-mony that are intrinsic to Navajo life.*

grueling. Those who wandered away from the column were often taken captive and enslaved by Mexicans. Hundreds of others were weak and ill, their systems in shock from dislocation and the strange foods they were offered along the way. "When the journey to Fort Sumner began, the Diné had hardly anything to comfort them or to keep them warm," a woman who had endured the Long Walk told her great-granddaughter decades afterward. "Women carried their babies on their backs and walked all the way, hundreds of miles."

When at long last the Navajo reached their new home, they were herded into a corral, counted, and given their first week's provi-sions—bacon, flour, and coffee. So unfamiliar were these items that some of the Indians mixed together roasted coffee beans and flour, or poured large quantities of baking powder into flour, then cooked it. The alkaline water further upset the Navajo's stomachs, and many developed dysentery. Perhaps most crippling of all was the overcrowding—huge numbers of people had been forced onto 40 square miles of arid land that was incapable of supporting them. By March 1865, there were more than 9,000 Navajos crammed into the Bosque Redondo. Here they were expected to build their homes—although there was hardly any wood available—and learn to plow and irrigate fields, so they might become self-sustaining.

For four years, the Navajo suffered miserably. With timber for hogans scarce, most of them lived in crude shelters carved out of the earth, with branches for roofs. Lacking firewood, they shuddered in the cold. So thin were the army-issue blankets that Navajo women—perhaps recalling how their mothers had unraveled Spanish bayeta for its brilliant red thread—patiently unwound the yarn and rewove it into a thicker and more durable cloth. Year after year, the Navajo crops failed—once from a blight of caterpillars, then again, and still again, from flood, hail, drought, and windstorm. So hungry were the prisoners of the Bosque Redondo that one survivor recalled seeing young boys scavenging a pile of horse manure for undigested kernels of corn, which they then cooked in hot ashes. It was abundantly clear to the Navajo that the Holy People did not wish them to live in this alien land.

By 1868 the federal government was forced to admit that General Carleton's scheme was both a financial and humanitarian disaster. Envoys went to Fort Sumner to negotiate with the Indians, hoping to persuade the Navajo to move to Oklahoma, where land had been set aside as Indian territory. At the meeting, Barboncito, one of several Navajo leaders in the Bosque Redondo, spoke for the People. "We do not want to go to the right or left, but straight back to our own country," he declared.

Barboncito spoke eloquently. According to Navajo legend, he was aided by the spirits, for, as he talked, he held under his tongue a turquoise stone sprinkled with pollen brushed off a coyote. Furthermore, the Navajo agreed to halt all raids against settlers and to send their children to government schools. The federal government readily agreed. On June 18, the Navajo left the Bosque Redondo. Although perhaps 2,000 people had died during the four years of war and exile, the survivors nevertheless formed a column some 10 miles long. A small portion of their former realm was set aside as the Navajo Indian Reservation, and the People began the long journey back to the wealth and prosperity they had once known.

Never again would the Navajo rove freely across the open range they had once owned. Nor would the sacred canyon land ever again be theirs and theirs alone. Yet, thanks to their adaptability, these remarkable people have regained their strength—today they are the largest Indian nation living in the United States, numbering some 200,000. Present-day Navajos, of course, are teachers, lawyers, doctors, miners, and factory workers, as well as farmers and sheepherders. Women continue to weave, although their products are generally sold to tourists, rather than fashioned into items for family use. Most important, the spiritual life of the People remains strong. A life based on harmony and happiness is still the Navajo ideal. To achieve this goal, Navajo singers continue to chant the Blessingway ceremony, retelling the story of the creation of the Navajo world in the land between four mountains, where the People dwell today. ❖

# THE DAWN OF AN APACHE WOMAN

Faced with the persistent threat of withering want and early death that the southwestern environment poses to its inhabitants, the Apache peoples have long believed that their vitality depends on the well-being of their women, the bearers of life and the embodiment of fruitfulness. Thus, the coming of age of an Apache girl is regarded by the members of her community as an event of supreme importance. Traditionally, it is celebrated with elaborate ceremony in what remains today as one of the most sacred rituals of the Apache world.

*Na'ih'es,* literally "getting her ready," or the Sunrise Dance as it is also called, typically takes place in the summer following a teenage girl's first menses. The four-day ritual relates in song and dance the story of Changing Woman, who according to legend was impregnated by the sun and gave birth to the Apache peoples. During the ceremony, the girl ritually dwells in a four-poled, tipilike arbor *(left)* that represents the deity's own home. With the help of a medicine man, she invites the spirit of Changing Woman to inhabit her body and invest her with the qualities she will need to lead a long and useful life.

For the community at large, the Sunrise Dance reinforces family and tribal connections and offers the opportunity to reap the benefits of Changing Woman's benevolence. "Walk with honor and dignity. Be strong," exhort the initiate's relatives and elders, "for you are the mother of a people."

*Four eagle feathers are strung across the sacred shelter to promote a long and healthy life.*

# THE MEDICINE MAN'S BLESSING

Months before the dance, the girl's family selects a site and starts to prepare dwelling and cooking areas to house and feed the horde of expected guests. A woman is selected as the girl's sponsor, and a medicine man is engaged to sing and to prepare ritual paraphernalia.

At sunrise on the first day of the ceremony, the medicine man blesses the initiate *(right)*. Then the girl, accompanied by her attendant, stands in front of the pile of blankets on which she is to dance *(opposite)*. Symbols of abundance—a buckskin, baskets of candy, and crates containing fruit and soft drinks—are arrayed before her.

*An abalone-shell pendant (left), worn on the initiate's forehead, is a symbol of her personification as Changing Woman, who according to Apache legend sought refuge under an abalone shell during a great flood.*

*The yellow buckskin ceremonial dress shown below, modeled after the garment said to be worn by Changing Woman, is the color of pollen, a symbol of fertility.*

## A TRANSFER OF GODLY POWERS

As she dances to songs that tell how Changing Woman helped shape the Apache world, the initiate faces the rising sun and kneels as the deity knelt when the sun impregnated her *(right)*. Praying to be endowed with Changing Woman's powers, the girl dances for as long as six hours at a stretch. Periodically, her sponsor *(Naa'il'eesn)* massages her to strengthen and mold her *(above)*. "Changing Woman's power is in the girl and makes her soft, like a lump of clay," explained one medicine man. "Naa'il'eesn puts her in the right shape . . . rubs her legs so she will never have any trouble walking long ways . . . her back so that when she gets to be really old she won't bend over . . . her shoulders so she can carry heavy things for her camp and never get tired."

*A ritual cane, decorated with eagle feathers to ensure health and oriole feathers for a good disposition, is made of hardwood in order to last into the girl's old age and support her when she becomes frail.*

# DRIVING AWAY EVIL

In the evenings, black-masked dancers, representing the benevolent mountain spirits called *gaan*, perform to drive away evil and guard against illness *(below)*. A white-masked clown, shown at left blessing

*A shallow basket is filled with the pollen showered over the girl. The short bristles on the grass brush are used to comb her hair; the long uneven bristles disperse the pollen.*

a guest, provides comic relief during the ritual, assists with controlling the crowd, and serves as a messenger for the other dancers, who are not permitted to speak.

Toward the end of the ceremony, the medicine man sprinkles cattail pollen, signifying fertility, over the girl's head. He then pours the contents of a small basket filled with candy, corn kernels, and coins over her—an act that sanctifies the contents of all the other baskets and cartons of food that have been assembled to distribute to the crowd. According to Apache tradition, those guests who receive a piece of candy from this bounty will always have plenty of food; those who keep and plant the corn kernels will reap abundant harvests; and those who acquire coins will become rich.

# A PLEA FOR COMMUNAL PROSPERITY

As the ceremony draws to a close, the pollen-covered girl and her sponsor dance in place, while guests line up to bless her—and to ask her to invoke Changing Woman's power to grant personal wishes. Then, in the ritual's final act, the girl shakes out her buckskin and blankets and casts them to the north, south, east, and west, affirming the ceremony's communal importance. Explained one Apache: "She throws the blanket so she can always have blankets, plenty of them, in her camp when she gets old. She shakes them out, like if they had dust in them, so her blankets and camp will always be clean. The buckskin she throws so there will always be deer meat in her camp and good hunting for everyone."

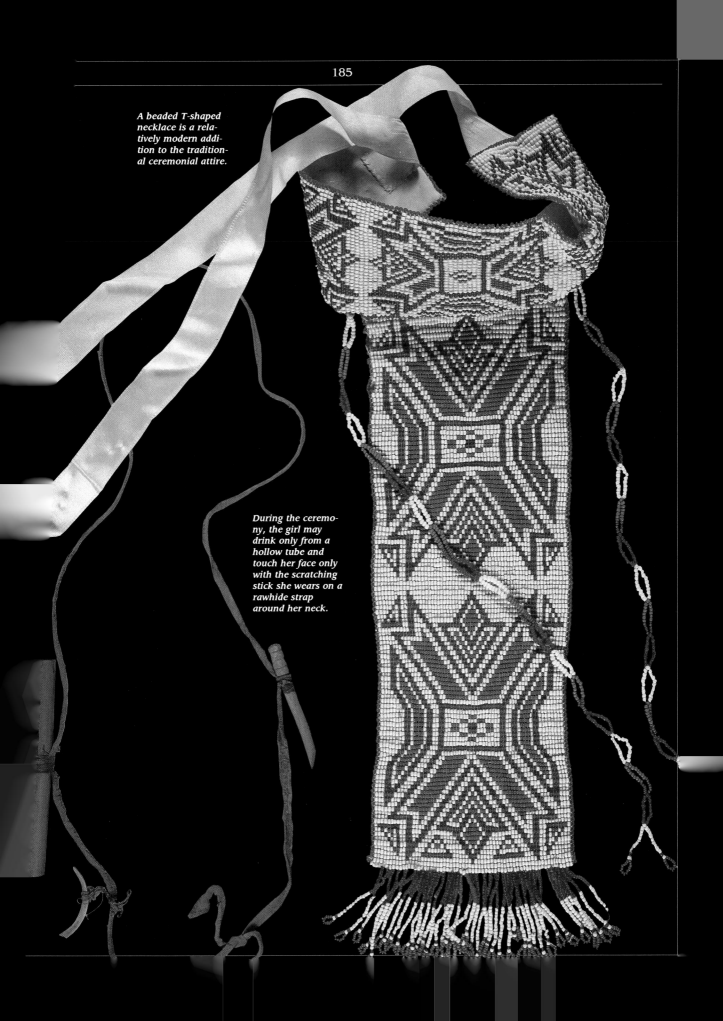

A beaded T-shaped necklace is a relatively modern addition to the traditional ceremonial attire.

During the ceremony, the girl may drink only from a hollow tube and touch her face only with the scratching stick she wears on a rawhide strap around her neck.

# ACKNOWLEDGMENTS

*The editors wish to thank the following individuals and institutions for their valuable assistance:*

*Arizona:* Flagstaff—Carol T. Burke, Museum of Northern Arizona. Phoenix—Barton Wright. Prescott—Michael J. Wurtz, Sharlot Hall Museum of Arizona History. Tempe—Patricia Etter, Hayden Library, Arizona State University. Tucson—Theodore R. Bundy, Diane Dittamore, Arizona State Museum; David Burckhalter; Mary Beck Moser; Emory Sekaquaptewa, University of Arizona. Whiteriver—Arthur

A. Guenther.

*California:* Los Angeles—John Cahoon, Natural History Museum of Los Angeles County; Michael Wagner, Southwest Museum.

*Colorado:* Denver—Cynthia Nakamura, Denver Art Museum.

*Oklahoma:* Tulsa—John R. Wilson.

*Nevada:* Reno—Chelsea Miller Goin.

*New Mexico:* Albuquerque—Krisztina Kosse, Natalie Pattison, Marian Rodee, Maxwell Museum of Anthropology. Corrales—Susanne Page. Santa Fe—Bruce Bernstein, Museum of Indian Arts and Culture;

Edmund Ladd, Arthur L. Olivas, Richard Rudisill, Museum of New Mexico; Eunice Kahn, Wheelwright Museum of the American Indian. Zuni—Jim Ostler, Pueblo of Zuni Arts and Crafts.

*Utah:* Salt Lake City—Stephen Trimble.

*Washington, D.C.:* Joyce Goulait, Nicholas J. Parrella, Museum of American History Photographic Services, Deborah A. Wood, Department of Anthropology, Smithsonian Institution.

*Wisconsin:* Milwaukee—Susan Otto, Milwaukee Public Museum.

*Wyoming:* Lander—Thomas Bowen.

# BIBLIOGRAPHY

BOOKS

Adair, John, *The Navajo and Pueblo Silversmiths.* Norman: University of Oklahoma Press, 1944.

Amsden, Charles Avery, *Navaho Weaving: Its Technic and History.* Chicago: Rio Grande Press, 1964 (reprint of 1934 edition).

Arthur, Claudeen, et al., *Between Sacred Mountains: Navajo Stories and Lessons from the Land.* Tucson: Sun Tracks and the University of Arizona Press, 1984.

Bahr, Donald M., et al., *Piman Shamanism and Staying Sickness.* Tucson: University of Arizona Press, 1974.

Bahti, Mark, *Pueblo Stories and Storytellers.* Tucson: Treasure Chest Publications, 1988.

Bailey, L. R., *The Long Walk: A History of the Navajo Wars, 1846-68.* Los Angeles: Westernlore Press, 1964.

Bancroft-Hunt, Norman, *The Indians of the Great Plains.* London: Orbis Publishing, 1985.

Bandelier, Adolph F., and Edgar L. Hewett, *Indians of the Rio Grande Valley.* Albuquerque: University of New Mexico Press, 1937.

Barry, Patricia, *Bandelier National Monument.* Tucson: Southwest Parks and Monuments Association, 1990.

Basso, Keith H.:
*The Cibecue Apache.* New York: Holt, Rinehart and Winston, 1970.
*Western Apache Language and Culture.* Tucson: University of Arizona Press, 1990.

Beck, Peggy V., Anna Lee Walters, and Nia Francisco, *The Sacred Ways of Knowledge, Sources of Life.* Tsaile, Ariz.: Navajo Community College Press, 1992.

Bee, Robert L., *The Yuma.* New York: Chelsea House Publishers, 1989.

Bennett, Noël, *The Weaver's Pathway: A Clarification of the ''Spirit Trail'' in Navajo Weaving.* Flagstaff, Ariz.: Northland Press, 1974.

Berlant, Anthony, and Mary Hunt Kahlenberg, *Walk in Beauty: The Navajo and Their Blankets.* Salt Lake City: Peregrine Smith Books, 1977.

Bowden, Henry Warner, *American Indians and Christian Missions: Studies in Cultural Conflict.* Chicago: University of Chicago Press, 1981.

Branson, Oscar T., *Fetishes and Carvings of the Southwest.* Tucson: Treasure Chest Publications, 1976.

Bunzel, Ruth L., *Zuñi Katcinas: Forty-Seventh Annual Report of the Bureau of American Ethnology to the Secretary of the Smithsonian Institution, 1929-1930.* Glorieta, N.Mex.: Rio Grande Press, 1973 (reprint of 1932 edition).

Buskirk, Winfred, *The Western Apache: Living with the Land before 1950.* Norman: University of Oklahoma Press, 1986.

Castetter, Edward F., and Willis H. Bell, *Yuman Indian Agriculture: Primitive Subsistence on the Lower Colorado and Gila Rivers.* Albuquerque: University of New Mexico Press, 1951.

Crumrine, N. Ross, *The Mayo Indians of Sonora: A People Who Refuse to Die.* Tucson: University of Arizona Press, 1977.

Culin, Stewart, *Games of the North American Indians.* New York: Dover Publications, 1975 (reprint of 1907 edition).

Curtis, Natalie, ed., *The Indians' Book: An Offering by the American Indians of Indian Lore, Musical and Narrative, to Form a Record of the Songs and Legends of Their Race.* New York: Bonanza Books, 1987.

Cushing, Frank Hamilton:
*The Mythic World of the Zuni.* Ed. by Barton Wright. Albuquerque: University of New Mexico Press, 1988.
*Zuni Fetishes.* Las Vegas, Nev.: KC Publications, 1990 (reprint of 1880 edition).

De Grazia, Ted, and William Neil Smith, *The Seri Indians: A Primitive People of Tiburón Island in the Gulf of California.* Flagstaff, Ariz.: Northland Press, 1970.

Dittert, Alfred E., Jr., and Fred Plog, *Generations in Clay: Pueblo Pottery of the American Southwest.* Flagstaff, Ariz.: Northland Press, 1980.

Dobyns, Henry F., *The Pima-Maricopa.* New York: Chelsea House Publishers, 1989.

Dockstader, Frederick J., *The Kachina and the White Man: The Influences of White Culture on the Hopi Kachina Religion.* Albuquerque: University of New Mexico Press, 1985.

Doyel, David E., ''The Transition to History in Northern Pimería Alta.'' In *Archaeological and Historical Perspectives on the Spanish Borderlands West.* Vol. 1 of *Columbian Consequences.* Ed. by David Hurst Thomas. Washington, D.C.: Smithsonian Institution Press, 1989.

Dutton, Bertha P.:
*American Indians of the Southwest.* Albuquerque: University of New Mexico Press, 1983.

*The Pueblos.* Englewood Cliffs, N.J.: Prentice-Hall, 1976.

Earle, Edwin, and Edward A. Kennard, *Hopi Kachinas.* New York: Museum of the American Indian, Heye Foundation, 1971.

*Earth Energies,* by the Editors of Time-Life Books (Mysteries of the Unknown series). Alexandria, Va.: Time-Life Books, 1991.

Felger, Richard Stephen, and Mary Beck Moser, *People of the Desert and Sea: Ethnobotany of the Seri Indians.* Tucson: University of Arizona Press, 1985.

Ferg, Alan, ed., *Western Apache Material Culture: The Goodwin and Guenther Collections.* Tucson: University of Arizona Press, 1987.

Fergusson, Erna, *Dancing Gods: Indian Ceremonials of New Mexico and Arizona.* Albuquerque: University of New Mexico Press, 1988.

Fewkes, Jesse Walter, *Hopi Snake Ceremonies.* Albuquerque, N.Mex.: Avanyu Publishing, 1986.

Fontana, Bernard L.:
*Of Earth and Little Rain: The Papago Indians.* Tucson: University of Arizona Press, 1989.
*Tarahumara: Where Night is the Day of the Moon.* Flagstaff, Ariz.: Northland Press, 1979.

Forbes, Jack D., *Warriors of the Colorado: The Yumas of the Quechan Nation and Their Neighbors.* Norman: University of Oklahoma Press, 1965.

Gill, Sam D.:
*Native American Religions: An Introduction.* Belmont, Calif.: Wadsworth Publishing, 1982.
*Songs of Life: An Introduction to Navajo Religious Culture.* Leiden, The Netherlands: E. J. Brill, 1979.

Green, Jesse, ed., *Zuñi: Selected Writings of Frank Hamilton Cushing.* Lincoln: University of Nebraska Press, 1974.

Harlow, Francis H., *Two Hundred Years of Historic Pueblo Pottery: The Gallegos Collection.* Santa Fe, N.Mex.: Morning Star Gallery, 1990.

Hegemann, Elizabeth Compton, *Navaho Trading Days.* Albuquerque: University of New Mexico Press, 1963.

Hewett, Edgar L., *Handbooks of Archaeological History.* Albuquerque: University of New Mexico Press, 1937.

Hewett, Edgar L., and Bertha P. Dutton, eds., *The Pueblo Indian World: Studies on the Natural History of the Rio Grande Valley in Relation to Pueblo Indian Culture.* Albuquerque: University of New Mexico Press, 1945.

Highwater, Jamake, *Ritual of the Wind: North Ameri-*

can Indian Ceremonies, Music, and Dance. New York: Alfred Van Der Marck Editions, 1984.

Hinton, Leanne, and Lucille J. Watahomigie, eds., Spirit Mountain: An Anthology of Yuman Story and Song. Tucson: Sun Tracks and the University of Arizona Press, 1984.

Hirschfelder, Arlene, and Paulette Molin, The Encyclopedia of Native American Religions: An Introduction. New York: Facts On File, 1992.

Houlihan, Patrick T., and Betsy E. Houlihan, Lummis in the Pueblos. Flagstaff, Ariz.: Northland Press, 1986.

Iverson, Peter, The Navajos. New York: Chelsea House Publishers, 1990.

James, H. L., Acoma: People of the White Rock. West Chester, Pa.: Schiffer Publishing, 1988.

Keegan, M. K., and Frontier Photographers, Enduring Culture: A Century of Photography of the Southwest Indians. Santa Fe, N.Mex.: Clear Light Publishers, 1990.

Keegan, Marcia, The Taos Pueblo and Its Sacred Blue Lake. Santa Fe, N.Mex.: Clear Light Publishers, 1991.

Kennedy, John G.:
The Tarahumara. New York: Chelsea House Publishers, 1990.
Tarahumara of the Sierra Madre: Beer, Ecology, and Social Organization. Arlington Heights, Ill.: AHM Publishing, 1978.

Kent, Kate Peck:
Prehistoric Textiles of the Southwest. Albuquerque: University of New Mexico Press, 1983.
Pueblo Indian Textiles: A Living Tradition. Santa Fe, N.Mex.: School of American Research Press, 1983.
The Story of Navaho Weaving. Phoenix: Heard Museum of Anthropology and Primitive Arts, 1961.

Kirk, Ruth F., Zuni Fetishism. Albuquerque, N.Mex.: Avanyu Publishing, 1988.

Kluckhohn, Clyde, and Dorothea Leighton, The Navaho. Cambridge, Mass.: Harvard University Press, 1946.

Laubin, Reginald, and Gladys Laubin, Indian Dances of North America: Their Importance to Indian Life. Norman: University of Oklahoma Press, 1977.

Mails, Thomas E.:
The People Called Apache. Englewood Cliffs, N.J.: Prentice-Hall, 1974.
The Pueblo Children of the Earth Mother. Vol. 2. Garden City, N.Y.: Doubleday, 1983.

Mather, Christine, Native America: Arts, Traditions, and Celebrations. New York: Clarkson Potter, 1990.

Maxwell, James A., ed., America's Fascinating Indian Heritage. Pleasantville, N.Y.: Reader's Digest Association, 1978.

Melody, Michael E., The Apache. New York: Chelsea House Publishers, 1988.

Mindeleff, Victor, A Study of Pueblo Architecture in Tusayan and Cibola. Washington, D.C.: Smithsonian Institution Press, 1989.

Nabokov, Peter, Indian Running: Native American History & Tradition. Santa Fe, N.Mex.: Ancient City Press, 1981.

Nabokov, Peter, and Robert Easton, Native American Architecture. New York: Oxford University Press, 1989.

Navajo Stories of the Long Walk Period. Tsaile, Ariz.: Navajo Community College Press, 1973.

Opler, Morris Edward:
An Apache Life-Way: The Economic, Social, and Religious Institutions of the Chiricahua Indians. New York: Cooper Square Publishers, 1965.
Apache Odyssey: A Journey between Two Worlds. New York: Holt, Rinehart and Winston, 1969.

Ortiz, Alfonso, The Tewa World: Space, Time, Being, and Becoming in a Pueblo Society. Chicago: University of Chicago Press, 1969.

Ortiz, Alfonso, ed.:
Southwest. Vol. 9 of Handbook of North American Indians. Washington, D.C.: Smithsonian Institution, 1979.
Southwest. Vol. 10 of Handbook of North American Indians. Washington, D.C.: Smithsonian Institution, 1983.

Page, Susanne, and Jake Page, Hopi. Ed. by Robert Morton. New York: Harry N. Abrams, 1982.

Parsons, Elsie Clews, Pueblo Indian Religion. Vol. 1. Chicago: University of Chicago Press, 1939.

Pennington, Campbell W., The Tarahumar of Mexico: Their Environment and Material Culture. Salt Lake City: University of Utah Press, 1963.

Rodee, Marian, and James Ostler, The Fetish Carvers of Zuni. Albuquerque, N.Mex.: Maxwell Museum of Anthropology, 1990.

Russell, Frank, The Pima Indians: Twenty-Sixth Annual Report of the Bureau of American Ethnology to the Secretary of the Smithsonian Institution. Washington, D.C.: Government Printing Office, 1908.

Sandoval, Richard C., and Ree Sheck, eds., Indians of New Mexico. Santa Fe: New Mexico Magazine, 1990.

Shaw, Anna Moore, A Pima Past. Tucson: University of Arizona Press, 1974.

Spicer, Edward H.:
Cycles of Conquest: The Impact of Spain, Mexico, and the United States on the Indians of the Southwest, 1533-1960. Tucson: University of Arizona Press, 1962.
The Yaquis: A Cultural History. Tucson: University of Arizona Press, 1980.

Spier, Leslie, Yuman Tribes of the Gila River. New York: Cooper Square Publishers, 1970 (reprint of 1933 edition).

Teiwes, Helga, Kachina Dolls: The Art of Hopi Carvers. Tucson: University of Arizona Press, 1991.

Tiller, Veronica E. Velarde, The Jicarilla Apache Tribe: A History, 1846-1970. Lincoln: University of Nebraska Press, 1983.

Time and Space, by the Editors of Time-Life Books (Mysteries of the Unknown series). Alexandria, Va.: Time-Life Books, 1990.

Toulouse, Betty, Pueblo Pottery of the New Mexico Indians: Ever Constant, Ever Changing. Santa Fe: Museum of New Mexico Press, 1977.

Underhill, Ruth M.:
Life in the Pueblos. Santa Fe, N.Mex.: Ancient City Press, 1991.
The Navajos. Norman: University of Oklahoma Press, 1956.

Webb, George, A Pima Remembers. Tucson: University of Arizona Press, 1959.

Webb, William, and Robert A. Weinstein, Dwellers at the Source: Southwestern Indian Photographs of A. C. Vroman, 1895-1904. Albuquerque: University of New Mexico Press, 1987.

White, Leslie A., The Acoma Indians: Forty-Seventh Annual Report of the Bureau of American Ethnology to the Secretary of the Smithsonian Institution, 1929-1930. Glorieta, N.Mex.: Rio Grande Press, 1973 (reprint of 1932 edition).

Whiteford, Andrew Hunter, Southwestern Indian Baskets: Their History and Their Makers. Santa Fe, N.Mex.: School of American Research Press, 1988.

Whiteford, Andrew Hunter, et al., I Am Here: Two Thousand Years of Southwest Indian Arts and Culture. Santa Fe: Museum of New Mexico Press, 1989.

Witherspoon, Gary, Language and Art in the Navajo Universe. Ann Arbor: University of Michigan Press, 1977.

Wright, Barton:
Hopi Kachinas: The Complete Guide to Collecting Kachina Dolls. Flagstaff, Ariz.: Northland Publishing, 1977.
Hopi Material Culture: Artifacts Gathered by H. R. Voth in the Fred Harvey Collection. Flagstaff, Ariz.: Northland Press and The Heard Museum, 1979.

Wyman, Leland C., Southwest Indian Drypainting. Albuquerque: University of New Mexico Press, 1983.

The Year of the Hopi: Paintings and Photographs by Joseph Mora, 1904-06. New York: Rizzoli, 1982.

Yue, Charlotte, and David Yue, The Pueblo. Boston: Houghton Mifflin, 1986.

## PERIODICALS

Breunig, Robert, and Michael Lomatuway'ma, "Kachina Dolls: Form and Function in Hopi Tithu." Plateau (Flagstaff, Ariz.), Winter 1983.

Forde, C. Daryll, "Ethnography of the Yuma Indians." University of California Publications in American Archaeology and Ethnology, December 12, 1931.

Gallagher, Marsha, "The Weaver and the Wool: The Process of Navajo Weaving." Plateau (Flagstaff, Ariz.), Winter 1981.

Kent, Kate Peck, "From Blanket to Rug: The Evolution of Navajo Weaving after 1880." Plateau (Flagstaff, Ariz.), Winter 1981.

Scotta, K. J., "Indians' Conference Calls for Unity on Sacred Issues." Tucson Citizen, May 29, 1992.

Wheat, Joe Ben, "Early Navajo Weaving." Plateau (Flagstaff, Ariz.), Winter 1981.

Witherspoon, Gary, "Self-Esteem and Self-Expression in Navajo Weaving." Plateau (Flagstaff, Ariz.), Winter 1981.

## OTHER PUBLICATIONS

"Eight Northern Indian Pueblos." Visitors Guide. San Juan, N.Mex.: Eight Northern Indian Pueblos Council, 1992.

"Elements of Design: The Influence of Oriental Rugs on Navajo Weaving." Museum Exhibition Catalog. Reno: Nevada Museum of Art, 1989.

"From This Earth: Pottery of the Southwest." Pamphlet. Santa Fe, N.Mex.: Museum of Indian Arts and Culture, 1990.

Wheat, Joe Ben, "The Gift of Spiderwoman: Southwestern Textiles, the Navajo Tradition." Museum Exhibition Catalog. Philadelphia: The University Museum, University of Pennsylvania, 1984.

# PICTURE CREDITS

*The sources for the illustrations that appear in this book are listed below. Credits from left to right are separated by semicolons; from top to bottom they are separated by dashes.*

**Cover:** National Anthropological Archives, Smithsonian Institution, Washington, D.C., photograph by Edward Curtis, photo. no. 75-11252. **6, 7:** © Jerry Jacka. **8:** Willard Clay. **9-11:** Stephen Trimble. **12:** © Jerry Jacka. **13:** Willard Clay. **14-17:** Stephen Trimble. **18:** Museum of New Mexico, photograph by T. Harmon Parkhurst, cat. no. 2326. **20:** Map by Maryland CartoGraphics, Inc. **21:** Doll from Laguna, New Mexico: made from wood and pigments. The Brooklyn Museum 03.325.3009, Museum Expedition 1903, Museum Collection Fund. **22, 23:** Museum of New Mexico, photographs by T. Harmon Parkhurst, cat. nos. 3895; 3938. **24, 25:** Museum of New Mexico, photograph by T. Harmon Parkhurst, cat. no. 3629. **27:** Stephen Trimble. **28:** Map by Maryland CartoGraphics, Inc. **29:** The University Museum Archives, University of Pennsylvania, neg. no. T4-413. **30:** © Paul Slaughter. **32, 33:** Art by Greg Harlin of Stansbury, Ronsaville, Wood Inc., inset Seaver Center for Western History Research, Natural History Museum of Los Angeles County. **34:** Southwest Museum, photograph by Adam Clark Vroman, N.20381. **35:** Susanne Page. **36, 37:** Courtesy Maxwell Museum of Anthropology, neg. no. 6415; Museum of New Mexico, photograph by J. R. Willis, cat. no. 42111. **40:** National Anthropological Archives, Smithsonian Institution, Washington, D.C., photo. no. 2332-B. **41:** The University Museum Archives, University of Pennsylvania, neg. no. T4-344. **42, 43:** Nancy Hunter Warren. **44:** George H. H. Huey. **48, 49:** Seaver Center for Western History Research, Natural History Museum of Los Angeles County; The University Museum Archives, University of Pennsylvania, neg. no. T4-408. **50:** Courtesy Museum of New Mexico, cat. no. 73438. **52, 53:** Art by Rob Wood of Stansbury, Ronsaville, Wood Inc., inset Seaver Center for Western History Research, Natural History Museum of Los Angeles County. **55:** Peabody Museum, Harvard University, photograph by Hillel Burger, photo. no. T98. **56:** The University Museum Archives, University of Pennsylvania. **57:** School of American Research Collections in Museum of New Mexico, photograph by Ben Wittick, cat. no. 16234. **58:** Smithsonian Institution, Washington, D.C., photo. no. 88-10601. **59:** Smithsonian Institution, Washington, D.C., photo. no. 88-10608—Smithsonian Institution, Washington, D.C., photo. no. 88-10606—Smithsonian Institution, Washington, D.C., photo. no. 88-10609; Smithsonian Institution, Washington, D.C., Museum of Anthropology, photograph by Michael Mouchette, courtesy Maxwell Museum of Anthropology—Smithsonian Institution, Washington, D.C., photo. no. 88-10610—Smithsonian Institution, Washington, D.C., photo. no. 88-10605. **60, 61:** Larry Sherer, Pueblo of Zuni Arts and Crafts, except bowl, from *Fetishes and Carvings of the Southwest* by Oscar T. Branson, Treasure Chest Publications, Tucson, Arizona, 1976. **62:** Millicent Rogers Museum, Taos, New Mexico. **64, 65:** School of American Research, cat. no. IAF P.94—School of American Research Collections in Museum of New Mexico, photograph by Ben Wittick, cat. no.

16443. **67:** Katherine H. Rust Children's Collection, Albuquerque, New Mexico, photograph by Guy Monthan from *The Pueblo Storyteller: Development of a Figurative Ceramic Tradition* by Barbara Babcock, University of Arizona Press, Tucson, Arizona, 1986. **68:** Museum of New Mexico, photograph by Wyatt Davis, cat. no. 44191—Douglas Kahn, School of American Research Collections in Museum of New Mexico, cat. no. 31959. **69:** Denver Art Museum, acquisition nos. 1932.343—1932.492; © Jerry Jacka, courtesy Museum of New Mexico. **70:** Blair Clark, School of American Research Collections in Museum of New Mexico, Museum of Indian Arts & Culture/Laboratory of Anthropology, cat. no. 19136/12; Douglas Kahn, School of American Research Collections in Museum of New Mexico, Museum of Indian Arts & Culture/Laboratory of Anthropology, cat. no. 11050—© Jerry Jacka, courtesy The Heard Museum, Harvey Fine Arts Collection. **72:** Courtesy Museum of New Mexico, cat. no. 4393. **73:** Courtesy Museum of New Mexico, cat. no. 90743. **75:** Damian Andrus, courtesy the University of New Mexico-Albuquerque, Maxwell Museum of Anthropology. **76, 77:** Courtesy private collection, photograph by Joseph Mora; © John Running. **78, 79:** © John Running (2); courtesy private collection, photograph by Joseph Mora. **80, 81:** Damian Andrus, courtesy the University of New Mexico-Albuquerque, Maxwell Museum of Anthropology (3), except photograph, from *Shadows on Glass: The Indian World of Ben Wittick* by Patricia Janis Broder, Rowman and Littlefield, Savage, Maryland, 1990. **82, 83:** Damian Andrus, courtesy the University of New Mexico-Albuquerque, Maxwell Museum of Anthropology; courtesy private collection, photograph by Joseph Mora (2); © John Running. **84, 85:** Damian Andrus, courtesy the University of New Mexico-Albuquerque, Maxwell Museum of Anthropology (2); Milwaukee Public Museum. **86-95:** Background W. Cody/Westlight. **86:** Rare Books and Manuscripts Division, The New York Public Library, Astor, Lenox and Tilden Foundations, photograph by Edward Curtis. **87:** National Anthropological Archives, Smithsonian Institution, Washington, D.C., photo. no. 57494. **88:** Rare Books and Manuscripts Division, The New York Public Library, Astor, Lenox and Tilden Foundations, photograph by Edward Curtis. **89:** Museum of New Mexico, photograph by Guy C. Cross, cat. no. 119173. **90, 91:** Museum of New Mexico, photographs by Edward Curtis, cat. nos. 144546; 143711. **92:** Sharlot Hall Museum. **93:** Museum of New Mexico, Santa Fe, photograph by Edward Curtis, cat. no. 143715. **94:** Museum of New Mexico, photograph by Frank A. Hartwell, cat. no. 71236. **95:** National Anthropological Archives, Smithsonian Institution, Washington, D.C., photograph by Frank Russell, photo. no. 2629. **96:** © Jerry Jacka, courtesy The Heard Museum. **98, 99:** Arizona State Museum, University of Arizona, photograph by Helga Teiwes, neg. no. C-28251. **101:** P. K. Weis, Tucson, Arizona. **102:** Arizona State Museum, University of Arizona, photograph by Helga Teiwes, neg. no. 25585. **106, 107:** Painting by Louis Valdez, courtesy U.S.P.H.S. Indian Hospital, Sells, Arizona, photograph by David Burckhalter; Southwest Museum, photographs by Schenck & Schenck (3); Arizona State Museum, University of Arizona, neg. no. 56501. **109:** National Anthropological Archives, Smithsonian Institution, Washington, D.C., neg. no. 2747-B

—Peabody Museum, Harvard University, photograph by Hillel Burger, photo. no. T1232a. **110, 111:** Salamander Books Ltd., London. **113:** National Anthropological Archives, Smithsonian Institution, Washington, D.C., neg. no. 2685. **114:** Arizona State Museum, University of Arizona, neg. no. C-105/35. **116-123:** John P. Schaefer. **125:** Arizona State Museum, University of Arizona, photograph by Helga Teiwes, neg. no. C-28246. **128, 129:** Susanne Page; Susanne Page, courtesy *Millennium: Tribal Wisdom & the Modern World* by David Maybury-Lewis, Viking Penguin, New York, 1992; Damian Andrus, courtesy the University of New Mexico-Albuquerque, Maxwell Museum of Anthropology—Susanne Page. **130:** The University Museum Archives, University of Pennsylvania, neg. no. G6-11945. **131:** National Anthropological Archives, Smithsonian Institution, Washington, D.C., neg. no. 2793-A. **134:** Arizona State Museum, University of Arizona, photograph by Helga Teiwes, neg. no. C-28245—DeGrazia Art and Cultural Foundation. **135:** David Burckhalter; National Anthropological Archives, Smithsonian Institution, Washington, D.C., neg. no. 31372-D—David Burckhalter. **136, 137:** Arizona State Museum, University of Arizona, photograph by Helga Teiwes, neg. no. C-28249; C-28250. **138:** Museum of New Mexico, photograph by Edward Curtis, cat. no. 76955. **141:** Reverend Arthur A. Guenther Collection—Damian Andrus, courtesy the University of New Mexico-Albuquerque, Maxwell Museum of Anthropology. **143:** Museum of New Mexico, photograph by Ben Wittick, cat. no. 16333. **144, 145:** © Paul S. Conklin. **146:** Photograph by Vincent Foster, courtesy School of American Research, cat. no. SAR 1983-8-2. **147:** The University Museum Archives, University of Pennsylvania, neg. no. S8-12808. **148:** National Anthropological Archives, Smithsonian Institution, Washington, D.C., photo. no. 76-6292. **151:** Museum of New Mexico, photograph by Ben Wittick, cat. no. 15899—The University Museum Archives, University of Pennsylvania, neg. no. T4-415. **152:** National Anthropological Archives, Smithsonian Institution, Washington, D.C., neg. no. 76-6090. **153:** National Museum of the American Indian, Smithsonian Institution, Washington, D.C., neg. no. 6/4597. **154:** Smithsonian Institution, Washington, D.C., photo. no. 78-10160. **155:** © Jerry Jacka, courtesy The Heard Museum. **156:** Denver Art Museum, acquisition no. 1953.420. **157:** Arizona State Museum, University of Arizona, photograph by Helga Teiwes, neg. no. C-20426L. **158:** Marcia Keegan. **161:** National Anthropological Archives, Smithsonian Institution, Washington, D.C., photo. no. 56957—Male God Impersonator Mask (Hastsebaka): made from hide, sinew, pigments, gourd, fur, and hair. The Brooklyn Museum 03.325.3903, Museum Expedition 1903, Museum Collection Fund. **162:** Navajo Wind Altar Snakes: made from wood, pigments, cotton, and feathers. The Brooklyn Museum 03.325.3776.1-4, Museum Expedition 1903, Museum Collection Fund. **163:** Navajo Wind Altar Prayer Board: made from wood, pigments, cotton, and feathers. The Brooklyn Museum 03.325.3776.5, Museum Expedition 1903, Museum Collection Fund. **164, 165:** National Anthropological Archives, Smithsonian Institution, Washington, D.C., photo. no. 2447—© Jerry Jacka. **167:** The University Museum Archives, University of Pennsylvania, neg. no. LS1512—Damian Andrus, courtesy the University of New Mexico-Albuquerque, Maxwell Museum of Anthropology. **168:** Millicent Rogers Museum, Taos, New Mexico—Damian Andrus, courtesy the University of New Mexico-Albuquerque, Maxwell Museum of Anthropology. **169:** The University Museum Archives, University of Pennsylvania, neg. no. T4-285c2. **170:** Tony Berlant, Santa Monica, California, inset Museum of New Mexico, photograph by Ben Wittick, cat. no. 16480. **171:** Natural History Museum of Los Angeles County—Damian Andrus,

courtesy the University of New Mexico-Albuquerque, Maxwell Museum of Anthropology. **172:** Damian Andrus, courtesy the University of New Mexico-Albuquerque, Maxwell Museum of Anthropology. **175:** Courtesy Wheelwright Museum of the American Indian, no. P1A-#21. **177:** P. K. Weis, Tucson, Arizona—David T. Vernon Collection, Colter Bay Indian Arts Museum, Grand Teton National Park. **178, 179:** P. K. Weis, Tucson, Arizona—Arizona State Museum, University of Arizona, photographs by

Helga Teiwes, neg. nos. C-28244; C-28237; P. K. Weis, Tucson, Arizona. **180, 181:** P. K. Weis, Tucson, Arizona (2); Arizona State Museum, University of Arizona, photograph by Helga Teiwes, neg. no. C-28236. **182, 183:** P. K. Weis, Tucson, Arizona, except bottom left, Arizona State Museum, University of Arizona, photograph by Helga Teiwes, neg. no. C-28238. **184:** P. K. Weis, Tucson, Arizona. **185:** Arizona State Museum, University of Arizona, photographs by Helga Teiwes, photo. nos. C-28240; C-28243.

# INDEX

*Numerals in italics indicate an illustration of the subject mentioned.*